D1500084

Education in the 80's:

PHYSICAL EDUCATION

The Advisory Panel

Fay R. Biles, Professor, Kent State University, Ohio

Phyllis A. Blatz, Teacher, Chaffey High School, Ontario, California

Mark E. Dean, Professor, Northern Illinois University, DeKalb

Robert E. Gensemer, Associate Professor and Director of Graduate Studies (Department of Physical Education and Sport Sciences), University of Denver, Colorado

Doris R. McHugh, Supervisor of Physical Education, Huntsville City Schools, Alabama

Carol T. Miller, Athletic Director and Physical Education/Health Education Instructor, Calvert High School, Prince Frederick, Maryland

Glenn M. Smith, Dean, School of Health, Physical Education and Recreation, University of Wisconsin, La Crosse

Herman Weinberg, Associate Professor, University of South Florida, Tampa

Thomas M. Vodola, Director, Project ACTIVE, Township of Ocean School District, Oakhurst, New Jersey

Education in the 80's:

PHYSICAL EDUCATION

Celeste Ulrich
Editor
University of Oregon

Classroom Teacher Consultant
Jeffrey L. McCarley
Buffalo, New York

National Education Association
Washington, D.C.

Stock No. 3159-8-00 (paper)
           3160-1-00 (cloth)

Note

The opinions expressed in this publication should not be construed as representing the policy or position of the National Education Association. Materials published as part of the NEA Education in the 80's series are intended to be discussion documents for teachers who are concerned with specialized interests of the profession.

Library of Congress Cataloging in Publication Data
Main entry under title:

Education in the 80's—physical education

  (Education in the 80's)
  Includes bibliographies.
  1. Physical education and training—Addresses,
essays, lectures. I. Ulrich, Celeste. II. Series.
GV341.E36   613.7'07   81-22296
ISBN 0–8106–3160–1   AACR2
ISBN 0–8106–3159–8 (pbk.)

Contents

Editor

Celeste Ulrich is Dean of the College of Health, Physical Education, Recreation, Dance and Gerontology at the University of Oregon, Eugene. She has published numerous books and articles on stress physiology, behavioral bases of human movement, and the significance and meaning of physical education.

Classroom Teacher Consultant

Jeffrey L. McCarley is a physical education teacher in Buffalo, New York.

Education in the 80's: Physical Education is truly an exciting and readable book that should prove invaluable to the physical educator. It is not only for the "now" physical education but also for the future. It is filled with practical, directly relatable guidance for the physical education teacher.

If we are to function or survive in our complex society, our mind and body must work together to form a complete individual. Celeste Ulrich creatively explores this idea in the opening chapter and convincingly concludes that our body must be sound to carry out the wishes of our mind.

Elizabeth Bressan's chapter, "Back to Basics," focuses not on a return to the basics but on what is for physical education an initial arrival. The author emphasizes that physical education provides people with basic but unique behavioral and developmental experiences. She skillfully outlines how physical education addresses the three basic and important needs of individuals: self-concept, by teaching individuals basic skills of balance, hand-eye coordination, and rhythm; self-esteem, by helping people feel competent to meet more complex motor challenges; and self-actualization, by helping people master specific activities of their choice.

During the 80's physical education will no longer be associated solely with perspiration; it will be a curriculum in which standards for everyday living are learned. Lynn Barnett foresees this in her chapter, "Play Patterns and Human Expression." To be a good sport, to be loyal, and to be honest are commonly advocated in the classroom. The playing field is a principal place in the school setting where the individual is under pressure to meet these standards. Play patterns teach a student how to adjust to others, how to compete, how to win, and also how to face failure. Play patterns help prevent shyness, timidity, and psychological withdrawal. Thus a student's play patterns are one of nature's best ways of preventing introversion and introspection.

Alexander McNeill gives much needed information in his chapter on how we as physical educators need to motivate students to participate in motor activities. During the 80's we will see a change in physical education, with emphasis being placed on physical fitness and cardiovascular conditioning. We all must realize that improvement in total fitness leads to more effective living.

"Curriculum Designs for Fulfilling Human Agendas" contains, I believe, something for every individual, teacher or student. We know that learning takes place when there is a change in the individual. This chapter begins with preschool and continues through postsecondary education, identifying many experiences under the school's control through which desirable behavior changes can be sought. The author's orderly arrangement of planned experiences fulfills the concept of a good curriculum for physical education.

Anne L. Rothstein's chapter on motor skill acquisition has convinced me that if motor skill acquisition in the 80's is to benefit from the decade before, we must make changes. We must incorporate methods of integrating research fragments within single areas, and we must use an overall framework to integrate findings across areas. To put it another way, the critical variables must be isolated and then integrated, as a way of controlling the knowledge explosion in motor skill acquisition.

I found Chapter 7, "The S/*: The Transcendent Experience in Sport," to be breathtaking. Study of the transcendental experience in sport as a form of the human potential movement is still in its infancy. The only means of ascertaining and measuring the experience are basically subjective (verbal description of perceptions and emotions). The lack of consistent objective measurement due to differences in culture and language leads to perceptual discrepancy and makes rational belief difficult. There is little doubt that the phenomenon of transcendental experience exists, as depicted by various individuals in sports. The author of this chapter believes that more investigations should be undertaken in the area of psychology, sociology, and history to pinpoint a means of measurement, and I agree.

Sports is becoming big business in the 80's, as the chapter on sanity in sports points out. A great deal of emphasis is being placed on the skilled athlete. As individuals' skills are highly developed for public demonstration, enormous changes occur: The physical education student becomes the athlete and the teacher becomes the coach. Coaches are employing practices that I believe are destructive to the educational scene, and schools are recognizing the public relations possibilities of athletics. As Celeste Ulrich and LeRoy Walker argue, during the 80's monies received from media contracts should be used to support the entire amateur athletic world, not only the select few.

In the chapter on human adaptation Linda Bain points out that it's the responsibility of the entire educational system to contribute to human adaptation in any society. Physical education, specifically, must provide success experiences and satisfaction for children with differing abilities. Helping children set personal goals, having them compete only within their ability level, helping them find their own solutions to problems, are some of the ways in which we, as physical educators, can help keep individual children from becoming embarrassed or frustrated. The 80's will require mutual support and concern among all people, and a well-designed physical education program can contribute to the development of these qualities.

In "Gym and Gender" the authors give a brief history of sexism in physical education, pointing out, for example, that Spartan female children and youth were expected to engage in physical activity in order to produce healthy males for the state. There can definitely be a change in the 80's, for, according to Title IX, "No person shall, on the basis of sex, be excluded from participation in, be denied the benefits of, or be subjected to discrimination under any education program or activity receiving Federal financial assistance."

The final chapter looks at physical education as it should exist in this decade. Celeste Ulrich notes that physical education is no longer confined to the physical fitness and endurance of yesterday's school or classroom. The field of physical education is becoming more diversified in that major fields of study are emerging, such as health education, recreation, sports, dance, safety, gerontology, and health sciences. These various areas are becoming a part of what the author describes as human activity for the total life cycle of the human, birth to death.

Each chapter is complete in itself, and each author has presented new insights that need to be applied to this decade. This book also offers universalities for those interested in the contribution of physical education to the betterment of the individual and the enhancement of society. Because physical education covers a broad area, guidance in the areas addressed in *Education in the 80's: Physical Education* is a most valuable aid for physical education teachers.

Jeffrey L. McCarley
Physical Education Teacher
Buffalo, New York

Education is an important planned intervention in human life. Its mission is the betterment of the individual and the enhancement of society. The school has been the usual arena in which this mission has taken place. In the past the school was a "square" box, devoted to the transmission of human heritage from one generation to the next via cognitive processes.

The twentieth century has sponsored mutations in traditional education. The box has assumed a multifaceted shape. Affective and motoric behaviors have been acknowledged in conjunction with the cognitive pattern, and the mission of schooling has been extended to accommodate human/environmental adaptation and the extension and creation of knowledge.

In this new arena of educational action physical education has been able to make a meaningful contribution. Moving from a reputation heavily overloaded with biological connotations and hygienic admonitions, physical education now concerns itself with the art and science of human movement and explores the mission of education via holistic approaches that are attentive to knowing, feeling, and acting.

This compilation of essays attempts to expose the "now" physical education. It presents a glimpse of what the decade of the 80's portends for the "budgeted" future. Each of the authors has addressed new understandings and woven them into a design of application that is discrete to the ideas explored but also offers universalities for those who are interested in the contribution of physical education to the betterment of the individual and the enhancement of society. It should be noted that ideas are theoretically based and it is up to the reader to translate theory into practice.

Using the dominant themes of the now physical education—movement, play, and fitness—the contributors have explored a wealth of ideas that should sensitize all educators to the inherent values of being in the body. Such holistic being, a state of general well-being, has the potential to offer an elan, a vitality of human purpose.

It should be noted that a deliberate effort has been made to accommodate the unusual needs of the exceptional individual into a mainstreaming concept. Thus the ideas presented address all individuals. There will always be those who cannot be accommodated, and for such people, exceptions and extensive program adaptations will have to be made. To explore such adjustments, a more extensive treatment of the handicapped theme must be undertaken.

To a large extent, education for the 80's has already been determined. Many of the mechanisms that will abet change are already in place. They are the "budgeted" future. The advent of the middle school, the use of sophisticated equipment and technology, the interaction with the community, and the articulation of formal education with careers, portend directions for the future. The catalytic agents that ameliorate change, money and prestige, are exasperatingly mutable. However, there is ample reason to believe that education will not return to its medieval profile and that in its twentieth century form, curriculum-based physical education will continue to make a meaningful contribution to human well-being.

Celeste Ulrich, Editor
University of Oregon

CHAPTER 1

Body Being: The "Now" Physical Education

Celeste Ulrich

In the past physical educators have subscribed to both education *of* the physical and education *through* the physical. Both relevant ideologies in their time have given way to new insights and concepts so that it is now possible to consider the *physical of education.* The newer concept reflects the acute realization that humans must be treated as whole entities. The education of *homo sapiens* must be mindful of the gamut of human behaviors, the cognitive, the affective, and the motoric. All people know, feel, and act as they grow and develop. To ignore any aspect of the totality of behavior is to have an incomplete understanding of human being and becoming.

As long as humankind subscribed to the trilogy of mind, body, and soul as separate and unique components, it was tempting to arrange that trilogy in a hierarchical pattern. Thus it was suggested for eons that the human soul is the highest form of being. The soul has been assumed to be that aspect of the living human that transcends life and has the ability to communicate with eternity. The exact makeup of the soul has never been described successfully, but it is projected that the soul is an ethereal extension of life that must be accepted through an act of faith. The soul of humans brings them, in description, closer to the angels than to the beasts.

Supporting the enrichment of the soul has been the mind. The mind, loosely identified as the brain and its neurological connections, has been considered the processing mechanism of human being. In the intricate and confounding pattern of knowing, sensory input is identified, catalogued, and stored. Long life enhances the data bank, as do varied and extensive experiences. Thus humans know and understand and then react accordingly. It has been assumed that, for the most part, formal education is concerned with the mind, for data are arranged in sequential patterns that aid assimilation and cataloguing. The process of feeding the data to the individual's neural system has taken a multitude of forms, but the end result has always been the expectation that the brain will be changed in some yet undefined physiological form and content. That change will result in measurable behavioral actions of increased sensitivity to knowledge. Thus, in formal education, does the school take on the awesome responsibility of promulgating the wisdom of humankind. It concentrates on "knowing" and thus is supposed to enrich the soul.

It has been suggested that the body could be thought of as the entity that houses both mind and earthly soul. It is also assumed that the body, as a precious receptacle, must be conditioned to be in fit form. Such biological fitness should produce an individual with an edifice worthy for behaviors of a high order, an order to produce human worth. Thus it has been usual to think of the body as the "temple" in which the person lives, a temple that must be kept operating at an optimal level of functioning.

As a temple or a receptacle, the body could well be treated as an object. It could be trained, administered to, altered, and even subjugated. It was the revered temple in which the thinking and feeling individual lived. Traditionally the training of the body was considered important to human life but only of minor importance when contrasted with the maintenance of mind and soul. True, the sound body might sponsor the sound mind, which in turn could contribute to the sound soul, but there was no doubt as to the relative importance of each component. The body was base, subject to carnal longings and needs for sustenance. The mind, on the other hand, employed reason to move the individual toward understandings for the higher good, and the soul permitted humans to transcend the physical and mental constraints of biological life and extend self into a nebulous system of eternity. Such eternity seemed important in a world that espoused a spiritual life after death.

Just as the education of the mind was the province of the educational institutions, so the training of the body was delegated to the gymnasiums. Although it was acknowledged that there was some interweaving of those two educational enterprises, it was usually accepted that the matrix was a loose weave, a weave that was influenced by genetic disposition, age, sex, and perhaps race. The training of the body became the responsibility of body trainers who later identified themselves as physical educators and who tended to ally themselves with medicine. Thus physical educators were often considered medical trainers, in contrast with other educators, who were considered teachers.

Only recently has there been a serious challenge to the concept of the human trilogy. That challenge has been most pronounced as philosophers have suggested that the body should be thought of not as object, but as subject. Such a revolutionary idea insists that the individual *is* body rather than residing *in* body. It is further postulated that the body can be considered "the radical root of reality." Such a concept supports the belief that there is "body being," and therefore the physical *of* education is as cogent to human development as the mental of education and the spiritual of education. The individual is considered in truly holistic terms and educated accordingly.

As physical educators approached the idea of body being, it became clear that it would be necessary to identify the patterns of education that would enhance body being. The old training patterns would no longer suffice, although they could continue to be used as tools of teaching. The new patterns enabled physical educators to continue in their concept of service, a teaching commitment that assumed a responsibility for human welfare and was significantly concerned with "good health."

The mutation of trainers to teachers and physical training to physical education insisted that practitioners direct attention to the core content of physical education in its new school base. There were long arguments about the meaning of physical education. Many proponents of fitness suggested that physiological integrity, especially a sound cardiorespiratory system, was the central focus of physical education. They contended that fitness training was a means to a noble and humanistic approach to "the good life."

The proponents of skill acquisition insisted that the processing of human activity that always led to fitness and ultimately to the good life was the unique core of concern of physical education. They contended that skill acquisition permitted gaming patterns to be understood. This group of physical educators insisted that play designs were essential in human existence as an antidote to work and as a technique of self-actualization. They suggested that the social dimensions of humans were best served through ludic understandings sponsored by sports and actual participation in those sports. Athletics was the epitome of the gaming experience. Physical education programs should be used to move as many people as possible toward gaming opportunities at some level of acquired skill. In addition, it was accepted that skill enabled individuals to initiate activity at their own choosing.

In the midst of the fitness-play debate, there stepped in a third group of physical educators who were convinced that neither the end product (fitness) nor the teaching modality used (gaming) was the appropriate core of concern of an academic discipline. They argued that the focus of physical education must be the art and science of human movement, suggesting that the usual movement forms employed by physical educators were those that involved sport, gymnastics, aquatics, and dance, and that from each of these forms, when individuals were willing to accept a physiological overload, fitness (physiological integrity) would result.

The idea of human movement being the core of concern of physical education took many practitioners by surprise. Such a notion insisted upon a change in teaching emphasis and the amassing of new knowledge. It also suggested that human movement patterns might extend beyond those traditionally employed by physical educators. There was apprehension about how such forms would be identified and whether such an extension might not "tread upon the toes" of other disciplines that were also concerned with motoric education. In addition, apprehension was manifested because there was no established language to describe human movement and only obtuse ways of recording motor activity. Many argued that human movement design was at the stage that music had been before the invention of the musical scale and its recording staff. However, the dogged persistence of those who were beginning to explore the phenomenon of movement resulted in interactions that had not taken place before. Athletes began to talk to dancers; gymnasts began to explore common concerns with swimmers and coaches; trainers and teachers began to be aware of the human movement potential. Philosophers added their insights to what was being identified as the "kinesiorium of knowledge," and psychologists began to express a keen interest in nonverbal language. Paradigms were established with regard to "motor learning," a new and tentative vocabulary was explored, and some definitive steps were taken to use notation systems already established to record human movement patterns. Physical educators focused their attention on a variety of understandings, understandings that explored the physiological results of human movement, that looked at the behavioral patterns sponsored by human movement, that were sensitive to the social cognates of human movement, and that were concerned about different techniques for teaching human movement. The body being had stressed the importance of movement to the individual's understanding of self and environments, and physical education was beginning to be recognized in the educational design for planned intervention in human understanding. The conceptual framework of physical education as the art and science of human movement is for the 80's acknowledged and accepted as the now physical education.

There persists the attempt to study human movement from traditionally oriented disciplinary perspectives. Thus we continue to be alert to such discrete ideas as the physiology of exercise, the sociology of sport, the psychology of dance, human growth and development, the philosophy of sport, the anthropology of play, the aesthetics of dance, nonverbal communication techniques, and aquatics bionomics. But there is also increased attention to and concern with the possibility of creating a structure for physical education that is centered on a productive discipline. It is proposed that such a discipline be founded in the concept of the *physical of education* as promoted by *being in the body*.

Such a notion must extend its boundaries beyond the school-age population and develop a "womb to tomb" concern for human movement. It appears that in the 80's physical education will temper its alliance with formal education and stretch its concerns into the community sector. Physical education will become an increasingly attractive marketable enterprise. Hence the extension of physical education into what is already being labeled physical recreation is an expected format. The use of the performing arts as a format for movement expression with an emphasis upon dance is another extra-educational venture. Because of the concern for wellness in the health sciences, physical educators will undoubtedly use the movement motif in specific areas such as physical medicine and in nonspecific areas such as community health projects and individual wellness assessment techniques.

All of these focuses will make use of the understandings of movement and meaning. Physical educators will reach for designs of humanism, for play patterns of expression, for fitness as a product of functional integrity. The designs will be structured by curriculum emphases that are attentive to motor skill acquisition and coping techniques. The influence of gender/sex differences and of the athletic establishment will continue to structure the design of the now physical education, but we will begin to see the slow eradication of some of the stark differences of the past—differences that limited opportunities offered to participants—and the promotion of a more global and encompassing understanding for human movement potential. Physical education will be less exclusive and more inclusive.

It would seem that the now physical education has finally come full circle, from the Hellenic concepts of philosophy and gymnastics as the root concerns for self-actualization; through attention to a hierarchical pattern of human understanding; to a specialized thrust that sought synthesis through analysis; to the current encompassing construct, again, of body being as self-becoming and of individuals assuming responsibility for the thoughtful employment of activity patterns that are sensitive to the nature, needs, and desires of participants.

Physical educators are now moving in quantum leaps instead of inching along the continuum of human understanding. In the everyday, nitty-gritty attention to the development of fitness concerns, or to the enhancement of performance skills, or to the expansion of concern for gaming techniques, it may be easy to forget that the focus in physical education is human movement. But just as surgery is but one aspect of medicine, just as computer technology is but one aspect of quantitative analysis, just as the English language is but one aspect of human communication, so sport, aquatics, gymnastics, and dance are but discrete forms of human movement, and so the study of physiology, sociology, history, philosophy, psychology, and sociology only offer encapsulated knowledge about a discrete mechanism in the wider area of human movement understandings. The physical of education is providing pieces for the jigsaw puzzle of human knowledge as a powerful contributor to self-understanding. Such understanding is only discerned in reference to what is known from the past and what is being discovered for the future. The 80's should be an era of richness for physical education as physical educators begin to understand truly that the head is attached to the body and both components together enable the spiritual transcendence that suggests completeness with the universe. Mind, body, and soul are no longer trinity. For the 80's they are unity.

CHAPTER 2

Back to Basics: *The Humanistic Agenda for Physical Education*

Elizabeth S. Bressan

It is difficult to imagine any discussion about the purposes of formal education in any social order that would not address the issues of fundamental skills, desirable competencies, or the relationship between individual needs and group requirements. Expressed concerns that many educational programs may have drifted away from such "basic" considerations and responsibilities have led to a demand for reassessment of both the content and the processes of schooling. Within such an evaluation it is critical that the aspect of the curriculum labeled physical education be examined to determine the nature and extent of its potential contribution to basic education. To excuse physical education from such scrutiny would be as untenable an educational decision as to eliminate it from the curriculum without fair hearing.

Physical education, when conducted according to the tenets of a humanistic agenda, may provide individuals with unique behavioral and developmental experiences in the "basic human need" areas of self-concept, self-esteem, and self-actualization. The content of physical education must not be regarded simply as a collection of activities, but rather as the performance of patterns of movement or, more precisely, as an individual participant's attempt to meet a motor challenge. It is in a personal effort to approach and encounter motor behavior challenges, that the development of an individual's self-concept and self-esteem may become

18

involved. It is in a personal effort to take motor behavior challenges and convert them into opportunities for joy and self-expression, that the potential for self-actualization emerges as an outcome.

Of course, many kinds of motor challenges may confront an individual. Any task that requires a management of the body in space can be considered to present a type of challenge. Driving a car, knitting, and snow skiing all meet this definition. But physical education is concerned only with those special patterns of movement that hold the ultimate potential for the humanistic ideal of personal development—self-concept, self-esteem, self-actualization.[1] Substantial historical evidence suggests that those special movement patterns fall into three broad classifications:[2]

1. Sport forms of motor challenges

2. Dance forms of motor challenges

3. Exercise forms of motor challenges.

It is in the structuring of participation in the sport, dance, and exercise forms of movement, then, that humanistic physical education proposes to contribute to individual development. In formal terms physical education becomes the learning of sport, dance, and exercise skills in order to help the emergence of self-concept, the acquisition of self-esteem, and the fulfillment of self-actualization needs. Three progressive phases in the physical education program have been designed to maximize this positive relationship between motor skill development and personal development:

1. Achieving control of motor performance, which relates to concerns for the development of self-concept

2. Achieving specific techniques of motor performance, which relates to concerns for the development of self-esteem

3. Achieving style in motor performance, which relates to concerns for self-actualization.

Each program phase is sensitive to a special aspect of personal development. It is with this careful attention to personal development that humanistic physical education would claim its rightful place in any school program on "the basics."

ACHIEVING CONTROL AND THE
DEVELOPMENT OF SELF-CONCEPT

Normal social and intellectual development is intricately related to sensory and motor experience.[3] Body image and self-perception—both dimensions of self-concept—are also rooted in individuals' initial experiences with the management of their bodies in space. With this recognition of the integrated nature of development and the pervading impact that early movement experiences may have upon self-concept, the first phase of a humanistic physical education program is focused upon each individual gaining basic control of motor performance.

Achieving control is a form of environmental coping that has as its focus—

1. the development of perceptual motor skills, which includes practice in performing simple motor skills that respond to some information or cues from the environment (skills such as balance, hand-eye or foot-eye coordination, and moving to a rhythm or beat);

2. the development of body awareness skills, which includes practice in performing basic motor skills that offer seemingly simple, yet profound, motor challenges (skills such as throwing, catching, kicking, traveling on different body parts, and making different body shapes to represent different ideas).

The emphasis in this program phase is on discovering what the body can do, where the body can go, how the body can move, and what different kinds of physical relationships the body can achieve. As an individual begins to gain control of motor performance, it is hoped that the perception of "the" body becomes one of "my" body, that the individual incorporates a holistic view of self into self-concept. Physical education can contribute still further to such personal development if learning experiences are designed in a progressive and individualized fashion so that participants are free to progress at their own rate and encounter motor challenges as problem-solving situations appropriate for their level of motor skill. Such a design, which is sensitive to feelings of self-worth and oriented toward success, is possible when teachers avoid introducing the social-evaluation pressures of competition or grading into this phase of physical education.

ACHIEVING SKILL TECHNIQUES AND THE DEVELOPMENT OF SELF-ESTEEM

As individuals achieve increasing degrees of skill in motor performance, a general feeling of environmental coping may expand toward feelings of real competence and belief in their ability to act effectively in response to challenging situations. The learning of sport, dance, and exercise skills enables an individual to engage in controlled movement settings where physical performance becomes concrete evidence upon which to base self-evaluation—one of the central dimensions of self-esteem.[4] Each sport, dance, and exercise form has its own particular set of skill techniques designed to meet successfully its own particular set of motor challenges. Because it would be impossible to gain skill in every movement form, humanistic physical education programs must select only certain forms for extended practice and participation. Although facilities, time, and finances often affect this selection, individuals should be given the opportunity to learn the skill techniques of at least one movement form from each of the following:

1. From the sport forms:
   a. a sport that emphasizes competition
   b. a sport that emphasizes self-evaluation
   c. a sport that emphasizes vertigo (a threat to balance or stability).

2. From the dance forms:
   a. a dance that emphasizes mimicry (imitation)
   b. a dance that emphasizes cultural expression
   c. a dance that emphasizes personal expression
   d. a dance that emphasizes successful display (communication of an idea or feeling to others).

3. From the exercise forms:
   a. an exercise pattern that emphasizes maintenance of a desired level of physical condition
   b. an exercise pattern that emphasizes an improvement to a desired level of physical condition
   c. an exercise pattern that emphasizes restoration to a previous level of physical condition
   d. an exercise pattern that emphasizes relief from some undesired physical condition.

Although some educators might believe that the exercise forms are appropriate only for the physically handicapped or ill-fit individual, it should be noted that the knowledge and experience gained by participating in exercise forms may provide all individuals with positive feelings about their ability to change and control their own physical condition. The different types of sport and dance forms structure the environment in distinctly different ways. As skill techniques are mastered, each performer becomes more effective and gains in self-confidence—still another dimension of self-esteem.

As with the first program phase of achieving control, the second program phase of achieving skill techniques requires a careful sequencing of learning experiences so that individuals are sufficiently challenged to grow, yet they encounter enough actual success that they are able to develop and maintain their personal dignity. The educational beauty of sport, dance, and exercise is that they are totally contrived environments with identifiable motor challenges. A knowledgeable physical educator can help foster the development of positive self-esteem based upon accurate self-perceptions by setting up an instructional cycle in which the practice of specific skills is followed by the chance to apply those skills in a real yet manageable sport, dance, or exercise context, which in turn necessitates and provides feedback for further practice, and so on toward mastery.

ACHIEVING STYLE AND SELF-ACTUALIZATION

The final phase in a humanistic physical education program is that of achieving style in motor performance, that is, achieving a level of skill proficiency that frees the individual from constant concentration on the mechanics of motor performance and opens up its potential as an aesthetic experience. Because a high level of skill is required to achieve style, few individuals are capable of this mastery in more than one or two movement forms. This implies that there must be an identification of preferences for certain sport, dance, or exercise forms and then the provision of further instruction and extended opportunities for practice and participation. It is entirely possible that some students, after achieving the skill techniques of performance, might prefer to pursue only the dance forms to the level of style, or only the sport forms, or only the exercise forms. Other individuals might select a combination of the forms while still others might choose to pursue self-actualization in other forms altogether rather than pursue it in movement. In this phase of the program the student must be given a choice, even if that means the student's dropping out of the program. No one can identify for another where or how feelings of self-actualization may be encountered.

The aesthetic potential in motor performance provides a rich source of personal meaning for many individuals. This potential has been proposed as a range of feelings that includes the following: [5]

1. Evocative elements, where some human life value such as courage or compassion is illustrated by a motor performance

2. Expressive elements, where a participant has mastered the skill techniques to the point where he or she takes on a special "energy" quality such as grace, lightness of touch, power with control, etc.

3. Intellectual beauty, where a participant meets the motor challenges of an activity in some clever, insightful, or innovative movement

22

4. Drama, where there is some contrived conflict or difficulty in meeting the demands of an activity and tension builds as the struggle between the participant and adversary elements continues to some point of climax and resolution

5. Unity, where the participant experiences feelings of total immersion or oneness in his or her own skill performance.

Although a school physical education program could not offer a wide variety of sport, dance, and exercise forms to this degree of mastery, it might be possible to offer a representative sample if public and community resources were used. As with the other phases of the program, concern for individuals' feelings of personal worth and respect for their right to make choices about their physical education would permeate this final phase.

THE HUMANISTIC AGENDA

Humanistic physical education may be conceived of as a motor skill learning program structured to promote the development of self-concept and self-esteem and the pursuit of self-actualization among its participants. The primary difficulty with this type of physical education is that of realizing its own idea. Although all of our motor development literature tells us that the best time to work on achieving control of motor performance is between the end of the infant growth spurt and the stabilization of hand and foot preference between ages five and seven approximately,[6] a systematic perceptual-motor and body management program is seldom provided for children in this age range. At this critical time in the development of self-concept, when carefully and individually designed motor challenges could make a significant and positive contribution, formal and regular physical education instruction is often totally absent. When some effort is made to organize children, it usually becomes a low-skill-level group-oriented activity that is oblivious to individual differences in motor development and the fragile nature of children's evolving self-concept.

Both motor development and integrated-development literature suggest that the best period for learning skill techniques is between the ages when hand and foot preference stabilizes and puberty begins.[7] This would clearly indicate that the elementary and middle school years should find a rigorous sport, dance, and exercise skill technique program receiving full emphasis as children discover their abilities to become competent as active agents in their environment. This self-esteem-oriented program phase should again allow for individual differences and reflect a sensitivity to children's needs for accurate self-perceptions in a nonthreatening, nonjudgmental environment. However, many programs for children in this age span consist of a few playground games in which highly motor-skilled or gifted children are allowed to predominate. Often individualized skill instruction in specific techniques is not provided, and sufficient practice time for developing these difficult skills is never built in to the school day. The potential gain in self-esteem available to all children from progressive improvement in meeting motor challenges is seldom realized.

The final phase of skill mastery or style in motor performance should be the province of the secondary or high school curriculum. Instead, many times the physical education program is a weak attempt to teach basic skill techniques to individuals who have yet even to achieve full control of their motor performance. No wonder that many older students become bored or disinterested in high school and many educators see little basic value in physical education. The lack of initial physical education during critical stages in development provides a nearly insurmountable obstacle. The opportunities for self-actualization in such developmentally out-of-sync programs are remote at best.

The humanistic agenda in physical education demands early intervention, as early as the preschool, in children's motor development. Throughout the entire program teachers must structure motor challenges for students that encourage a steady expansion of their capabilities in a nonthreatening learning environment. Throughout the entire program teachers must provide skill instruction and guided practice that allow children to progress at their own rate without fear of unwarranted social evaluation or arbitrary assignment of some external judgment about the comparative worth of their performance.

But support for humanistic physical education has yet to be mobilized in education. Perhaps this can be traced to some latent feelings about the medieval concept of mind-body dichotomy, which relegated anything concerning the physical to a position of secondary value. Perhaps it can be traced to an unwillingness to see participation in sport, dance, and exercise forms as a potentially meaningful pursuit for everyone from the handicapped to the highly gifted, because the acceptance of such a position might threaten the athletic power structure that is interested in using instructional and practice time only for a select few who play in sports that the public finds entertaining.

A humanistic physical education program defines its educational value in terms of its contribution to the basic human needs for personal development in the areas of self-concept, self-esteem, and self-actualization. If the catch phrase "back to basics" is ever fully employed to effect curriculum change, the idea of humanistic physical education may at last be realized—a rich developmental experience in the real environments of sport, dance, and exercise. For physical education this will represent a true educational breakthrough, for it will not be a return to the basics, but rather an initial arrival, long anticipated by responsible physical educators and long deserved by their students.

REFERENCES

1. Hellison, D. *Humanistic Physical Education*. Englewood Cliffs, N.J.: Prentice-Hall, 1973.

2. Metheny, E. *Movement and Meaning*. New York: McGraw-Hill, 1968.

3. Harris, D. *Involvement in Sport*. Philadelphia: Lea and Febiger, 1973.

4. Jersild, A. *In Search of Self*. New York: Teachers College Press, 1952.

5. Carlisle, R. "Physical Education and Aesthetics." In *Readings in the Aesthetics of Sport*, edited by H. T. A. Whiting and D. W. Masterson. London: Lepus Books, 1974.

6. Corbin, C. *A Textbook of Motor Development*. 2nd ed. Dubuque, Iowa: Wm. C. Brown, 1980.

7. Arnold, P. *Education, Physical Education and Personality Development*. London: Heinemann, 1968.

CHAPTER 3

Play Patterns and Human Expression

Lynn A. Barnett

*"A human is most human . . . when at play."**

INTRODUCTION

All of us have engaged in a wide variety of play since our earliest months. As infants, we found delight in touching a colorful mobile and tittered at the sight of adults retrieving dropped spoons. As young children, we built spaceships and cities from grains of sand, and we learned skills for gaming and the fun that others could bring. And as adults, we have often retreated into dreams of childhood play or engulfed ourselves for hours in conversations to solve world problems and in mutual expression via interpersonal relationships. Play provides unique opportunities for the individual: it relaxes us from daily toil, allows us to conjure up dreams of "what could be" or "what was," provides nonserious experimentation with our universe, and generally yields a state of pleasure, satisfaction, and enjoyment that few other activities bring. For all of these opportunities and accomplishments, play is the mechanism by which we express ourselves freely, with the latitude and freedom to act on our gratifications and wishes and bear no consequences.

The freedom to choose, to act, to express, to feel, is a defining characteristic of play. The intrinsic motivation that characterizes playful

---

*Ellis, M.J. *Why People Play.*

initiations carries positive emotional responses as we engage in actions for the internal gratification they elicit. In few other behaviors do we perceive the contingencies attached to our acts to be so minimal, the consequences to be so relatively few. It is this perception of freedom that allows the individual to act with intent, the act itself being characteristic of internal states and dispositions. Play thus can be viewed as a sort of "looking glass" into the individual: it is the unique expression of moods, desires, personality, mental processes, and abilities and is a composite reflection of the individual—past, present, and future.

PLAY AS PHYSICAL EXPRESSION

Various theoretical views suggest that play is the expenditure [1] or the restitution [2] of energies that are either accumulated or discharged during working behavior. These early models thus define play as nonproductive, and superfluous and antithetical to work or purposive activity. Observations of the exuberant and vigorous play of children suggest some anecdotal support for the paradigms. [3] Indeed, gross motor activities have been found to characterize a majority of play styles in middle childhood, especially in boys. [4] Preschoolers and kindergartners show high degrees of physical experimentation in play as they learn to coordinate body movements and muscular activity. The precarious balancing feats that children often attempt (much to the dismay of parents) suggest that play serves as one means by which children learn the boundaries of their physical capabilities and coordination of body units to interact in new types of games. The perfection of these movements and the development of their patterns into skilled action often preoccupy much of play. [5] Play thus serves a critical function in providing children with the freedom to experiment with their body physically and relate it to interactions with their environment. The feedback gained during this type of play is crucial to children as they learn to integrate muscle groups, develop motoric patterns into skilled action, and discover the many new ways in which these newly acquired skills can bring efficiency in adapting to and manipulating their environment.

PLAY AS SOCIAL EXPRESSION

The development of social play has received a good deal of attention. Longitudinal observations of children at play have produced developmental stages, or categories, of social play. It is generally accepted that solitary play, followed by parallel play, associative play, and, finally, cooperative play is the sequence in which social play develops with age.[6] The social life of a child actually begins at birth. The child could not survive without being cared for, and this involves innumerable contacts with other humans from the start. When the child is between five and seven months old, he or she will laugh in fairly rudimentary games, and after a few more weeks the child will take an active part in the games.[7] After the first year a good deal of play is initiative. Other children are a great attraction as infants get older. Although there is considerable variation, some children as young as two-and-a-half years will appear distraught among a group of attractive toys if there are no others with whom to play. Most children in the first two years, however, when in close proximity, will play without much reference to others around them. Playing in parallel, rather than with one another, was found to be the most prevalent social-play form between the second and third year. Children appear to delight in others playing around them, yet they have little direct influence on the typology of one another's play. Associative play occurs a bit later when the child is engaged in a game involving others, yet is more intent on his or her own role and play interests. The appearance of cooperation is exceptionally rare before the age of three and does not actually govern play until five to seven years. Along with cooperative play goes competition, and these play styles are most readily observed in games and playful activities with high elements of imposed structure.[8]

The role of play in the child's socialization has been an important area for research activity. Play has been described as a key agent in the socialization process, as one of the means by which young children learn their role in relation to others and to the world in general.[9] From a young age children imitate adults: facial, verbal, and motoric actions; events witnessed and, at a later age, events heard of rather than experienced. Children learn what others in their society do, and are given feedback on their responses. Actions that are not culturally appropriate are punished and those that conform to social rules are positively reinforced. Children thus begin to internalize normative systems—for their culture, their society, their gender, and their immediate familial environment. This is one of the means by which our culture is transmitted from generation to generation. From a very early age we reenact culturally prescribed actions.

As children become outer-directed, that is, as their egocentrism gives way to an awareness of peers and the consideration of their peers' role in relation to their own, they acquire a general sense regarding the consequences of their actions in relation to others.[10] Before the age of two, outbursts of anger are directed mainly against adults, but between the ages of three and four quarreling with other children takes precedence.[11] This is the time when playmates gain importance, and as this occurs children begin to learn the meaning of sharing and cooperation. Like most other socially desirable habits, sharing is learned via a variety of incentives and social pressures. Sharing toys and taking turns, two essentials in reducing quarrels, are learned by experience. Through early adult intervention children learn the enjoyment that can be gained through interaction with others, and peers become a new toy form. Crucial to this process is children's realization that their own wishes cannot always predominate, and that gratification can be derived from subordinating their own desires to those of others. Piaget [12] stressed the internalization of morality and the development of conscience that can be traced through this process of recognizing the needs and wants of peers. He illustrated this relationship by tracing the game of marbles and the way in which children structured rules based upon group consensus. Play thus serves an important role in the socialization process via the continual enjoyable interactions between children and adults and, later, between children and other children.

It has also been suggested that communication skills, both verbal and nonverbal, are facilitated in play. [13] At a very early age (usually six to ten months) children begin to experiment with language: babbling and vocal noises are common and there is evidence that children begin to play with vocal sounds. [14] Between the ages of two and three years conventional noises are learned and used to identify certain events and actions. As more and more verbalizations accompany play, they elicit responses, whether or not they are clearly identifiable. The child's play with language is a common event in its own right, as chants, rhymes, and riddling songs emerge and produce delight. This type of language play often evolves into instructional games, with adults frequently mimicking and directing the content. These play episodes become important ways of teaching children labels and categories as well as the structural rules of language. The nonverbal accompaniments reinforce the joy in producing sounds and the ecstasy of initial success in communicating needs or identifying an object or person. The potential impact of nonverbal gestures becomes realized as a means of eliciting reaction or communicating feelings and thoughts.

PLAY AS COGNITIVE EXPRESSION

One of the most pervasive play styles in young children is the active investigation and manipulation of objects and settings. The child's seemingly insatiable curiosity in the preschool period is witnessed by parents and educators; the mischievous exploration of kitchen cupboards and the interminable frequency of "why" questions are characteristics of this period of rapid growth and development. The finding that raw construction materials are the most preferred play object in this age range[15] attests to the ingenuous ability of children to create fantastic characters and weave elaborate plots and themes. Dress-up play and the adventurous missions of young space cadets illustrate the manipulation of reality that is so typically characteristic of young children's play.[16] Like children, adults create make-believe or "wish" worlds, although typically these are covert, not overt. Research has shown that not only is this type of mental play quite enjoyable for those who participate, but it is also biologically adaptive; that is, imaginative play and playmates serve definite cognitive functions.[17]

A wealth of research illustrates a relationship between children's frequency of imaginative play and various aspects of cognitive development.[18] Piaget[19] suggested that play serves as the mirror through which we can observe the child's present level of cognitive functioning. More recently it was shown that children who exhibited high incidences of imaginative play in preschool years performed better in school subjects that those who had been more conventional in their play.[20] Creative children have been found to show advanced levels of reading comprehension and skill by first and third grade[21] and to produce more analytic concepts than their less playful peers.[22] Enhancing the child's ability to see the fun in learning, and structuring the traditional classroom setting into a more game-like atmosphere facilitate the acquisition of new concepts. Researchers have tested this notion experimentally by incorporating mathematical principles into a new game that was taught to grade-school children. The findings indicated that the children who participated in the new game acquired the concepts earlier and retained them longer than those who were taught via more conventional, structural approaches.[23] In addition, standardized tests that are traditionally administered to grade-school children achieved better results when the setting was less structured and was presented as a new game to be played.[24]

Theoretical models have been advanced to suggest that the very nature of play lies in cognitive processing.[25] The suggestion has been that the increases in language, reading, mathematical abilities, and other areas that have been noted are all reflective of problem-solving and divergent-thinking ability. The explanation for these findings is that children will typically explore and manipulate a novel object in their environment until they learn its characteristics. Once they feel familiar with an object, they will often creatively manipulate it, that is, generate new stories and situations with it.[26] In this way children learn the many possibilities that an object offers. The frequency with which this manipulation typically occurs throughout childhood leads to the development of a general problem-solving ability. As children investigate objects and learn the characteristics of those objects, they increase their response repertoire, and as they tire of the objects, they seek new interactions in their environment. These new interactions are of a necessarily more complex nature as children become more complex through increasing investigation, manipulation, and assimilation of aspects of their environment. Play thus contributes to children's adaptation to the world, as new information is learned and behavioral flexibility is acquired.

PLAY AS EMOTIONAL EXPRESSION

Sigmund Freud [27] long ago identified the adaptive value of play for the child. He argued that children do not have the means with which to assimilate unpleasant experiences, as adults do. Various defense mechanisms that adults possess to deal with conflicts posed by their environment are not fully developed in the young, and hence children require a means by which they can "digest" traumatic events. Play is regarded as one of the few activities in which the child has freedom for total control and direction. Children frequently use this control to reenact unpleasant experiences so as to insulate themselves from the effects of subsequent similar experiences in which they might once again have little control.

The importance of play behaviors to anxious or disturbed children has been demonstrated. In one study [28] school-age children who were hospitalized for a serious illness were presented with a variety of toys with which they could play. The children played for longer periods of time with the toys that closely resembled aspects of the hospital setting. The investigator also spoke with the children about their toy preferences and their feelings accompanying play. All of the children reported their play to have had a calming yet highly enjoyable effect, and the desire to continue the play activities was commonly expressed. In a more recent study [29] this psychoanalytic interpretation of play was studied in a controlled setting. One group of preschool children was shown a film segment from a Lassie movie that depicted Lassie getting separated from her owner and getting lost trying to find her way home. The dog's fate was uncertain as she encountered several potentially dangerous situations. This film segment was deemed to be anxiety inducing for the children. A second group of children was shown film segments from the same movie in which the dog made friends with a group of boys; this situation was pleasant and there was no indication of the dog's plight. After viewing their respective film segments, the children were given the opportunity to play individually with one or all of a variety of toys, some of which were relevant to the theme of the movie and some of which were neutral and bore no relation

31

to it. Measures of anxiety were taken for each child before and after the film and at the conclusion of the play session. Results supported the contention that play enables the child to neutralize and work through a conflict situation. The children who viewed the traumatic film segment played substantially longer with the anxiety-relevant toys than did the second group; in addition, compared with the second group, they were higher in anxiety following the movie and lower in anxiety following the play session.

This research lends further credence to the notion that play can contribute to stable and healthy emotional development in children. Although there is little evidence (beyond that cited above) to substantiate this notion, it is common to see young children playing doctor to a sick doll, or parent to a group of younger neighbors. One interpretation of this play is that the child is actually recreating an unpleasant experience in an attempt to master and neutralize it.

CONCLUSION

"The play of children at times may strike us as fragile and charming, rowdy and boisterous, ingenuous, just plain silly, or disturbingly perceptive in its portrayals of adult skilled actions and attitudes." [30] Recent research has shown, however, that with the variety of play forms, the diversity of play patterns, and the multitude of play expressions, we should view play as crucial to healthy development. Without a concerted period of play in our young and developing years, we would not cope well with the complexity of adulthood and the necessary demands for creative thought, physical prowess, and emotional and social stability. Indeed, play helps children come to understand their world. It also provides the freedom to explore and the enjoyment to act as a unique expression of the composite picture of ourselves.

Play allows us to realize the intrinsic possibilities that our environment offers and gives us the freedom to explore our potential in non-threatening ways. Alternately it teaches us the boundaries and the guidelines that we must learn in order to live cooperatively with others and to share new experiences and dreams. Play is almost paradoxical in this sense—we experience the fun in learning, creating, achieving, and reacting and the sorrow in the constraints necessarily imposed by reality and society as we age. We learn to be effective within our environment, yet we also learn that we are accountable to others who share our social system. The conflicts that are engendered, and the joy that accompanies mastery, are crucial components to play experiences, and to adaptation in general.

Play helps us to advance cognitively as we explore novel elements in our environment and then use them in ways to satisfy our pleasures. Play teaches us the joy to be gained from others and the mode by which we must learn to accept and communicate. Play facilitates the resolution of conflict and reduces our anxieties as we act on and "play out" events that acted on and disturbed us. Play allows for the expression of physical exuberance, the sheer joy that accompanies vigorous exercise, and the development of coordinated movement and skilled action. In all of these ways play is not just frivolous or silly—it is biologically adaptive, productive behavior that molds us into constituents of a culture yet allows us the enjoyment of expressing our individuality and uniqueness. Clearly, then, we play because we are human and we are human because we play.

REFERENCES

1. Groos, K. *The Play of Animals*. Translated by E. L. Baldwin. New York: Appleton, 1898.

Spencer, H. *Principles of Psychology*. New York: Appleton, 1896.

2. Patrick, G. T. W. *The Psychology of Relaxation*. Boston: Houghton Mifflin, 1966.

3. Groos, K. *The Play of Man*. Translated by E. L. Baldwin. New York: Appleton, 1901.

Gulick, L. "Some Psychical Aspects of Physical Exercise." *Popular Science Monthly* 58 (1898): 793–805.

Gulick, L. "Interest in Relation to Muscular Exercise." *American Physical Education Review* 7 (1902): 57–65.

Millar, S. *The Psychology of Play*. Baltimore: Penguin, 1968.

4. Cockrell, D. "A Study of the Play of Children of Preschool Age by an Unobserved Observer." *Genetic Psychology Monographs* 17 (1935): 377–466.

Hurlock, E. B. "Experimental Investigations of Childhood Play." *Psychological Bulletin* 31 (1934): 47–66.

5. Beach, F. A. "Current Concepts of Play in Animals." *American Naturalist* 79 (1945): 523–554.

Loizos, C. "Play in Mammals." In *Play, Exploration and Territory in Mammals. Symposia of the Royal Zoological Society*, edited by P. A. Jewell and C. Loizos. London: Academic Press, 1966.

6. Bott, H. "Observation of Play Activities in a Nursery School." *Genetic Psychology Monographs* 4 (1928): 44–88.

Gesell, A. *The First Five Years of Life*. London: Methuen, 1955.

Ireland, R. "The Significance of Recreational Maturation in the Educational Process: The Six 'Ages of Play.'" *Journal of Educational Sociology* 32 (1959): 356–360.

Iwanaga, M. "Development of Interpersonal Play Structure in 3-, 4-, and 5-Year-Old Children." *Journal of Research and Development in Education* 6 (1973): 71–82.

Piaget, J. *Play, Dreams and Imitation in Childhood*. New York: Norton, 1962.

7. Buhler, C. "The Social Behavior of Children." In *The Evolution and Growth of Human Behavior*, edited by N. Munn. New York: Harrap, 1965.

Gesell, A., and Thompson, H. *Infant Behaviour: Its Genesis and Growth.* New York: McGraw-Hill, 1934.

8. Bruner, J., and Sherwood, V. "Peekaboo and the Learning of Rule Structures." In *Play: Its Role in Development and Evolution,* edited by J. Bruner, A. Jolly, and K. Sylva. Harmondsworth, England: Penguin, 1976.

Opie, I., and Opie, P. *Children's Games in Street and Playground.* New York: Oxford University Press, 1969.

9. Eifermann, R. "Free Social Play: A Guide to Directed Playing." In *Developing Motivation in Children,* edited by S. Coopersmith. Columbus: Merrill, 1972.

Garvey, C. *Play.* Cambridge, Mass.: Harvard University Press, 1977.

Parten, M. "Social Play Among Preschool Children." *Journal of Abnormal and Social Psychology* 28 (1933): 136–147.

10. Bronson, W. "Developments in Behavior with Agemates During the Second Year of Life." In *Peer Relations and Friendship,* edited by M. Lewis and L. Rosenblum. New York: Wiley, 1975.

Eckerman, C.; Whatley, J.; and Kutz, S. "The Growth of Social Play with Peers During the Second Year of Life." *Developmental Psychology* 11 (1975): 42–49.

Smith, P., and Connolly, K. "Patterns of Play and Social Interaction in Preschool Children." In *Ethological Studies of Child Behavior,* edited by N. Blurton-Jones. Cambridge, England: Cambridge University Press, 1972.

11. Goodenough, F. L. *Anger in Young Children.* Minneapolis: University of Minnesota Press, 1931.

12. Piaget, J. *The Moral Judgement of the Child.* Glencoe, Ill.: Free Press, 1948.

13. Garvey, C. "Some Properties of Social Play." *Merrill-Palmer Quarterly* 20 (1974): 163–180.

Opie, I., and Opie, P. *The Lore and Language of Schoolchildren.* New York: Oxford University Press, 1959.

Reynolds, P. "Play, Language and Human Evolution." In *Play: Its Role in Development and Evolution,* edited by J. Bruner, A. Jolly, and K. Sylva. Harmondsworth, England: Penguin, 1976.

14. Garvey, C. *Play. op. cit.*

15. Bott, H. "Observation of Play Activities in a Nursery School." *op. cit.*

Cockrell, D. "A Study of the Play of Children of Preschool Age by an Unobserved Observer." *op. cit.*

Hurlock, E. B. "Experimental Investigations of Childhood Play." *op. cit.*

16. El Konin, E. "Symbolics and Its Functions in the Play of Children." *Soviet Education* 8 (1966): 35–41.

Piaget, J. *Play, Dreams and Imitation in Childhood. op. cit.*

17. Griffiths, R. *A Study of Imagination in Early Childhood.* London: Kegan-Paul, 1935.

Jersild, A.; Markey, F.; and Jersild, C. "Children's Fears, Dreams, Wishes, Daydreams, Likes, Dislikes, Pleasant and Unpleasant Memories." *Child Development Monographs* 12 (1933): (whole issue).

Schaefer, C. "Imaginary Companions and Creative Adolescents." *Developmental Psychology* 1 (1969): 747–749.

Sperling, O. "An Imaginary Playmate Representing a Pre-stage of the Superego." *Psychoanalytic Study of the Child* 9 (1954): 252–258.

34

18. Fink, R. "The Role of Imaginative Play in Cognitive Development." *Psychological Reports* 39 (1976): 895–906.

Lieberman, J. N. *Playfulness: Its Relationship to Imagination and Creativity*. New York: Academic Press, 1977.

Pulaski, M. A. "Toys and Imaginative Play." In *The Child's World of Make-Believe*, edited by J. Singer. New York: Academic Press, 1973.

Sutton-Smith, B. "The Role of Play in Cognitive Development." *Young Children* 22 (1967): 159–160.

19. Piaget, J. *Play, Dreams and Imitation in Childhood. op. cit.*

20. Hutt, C., and Bhavnani, R. "Predictions from Play." *Nature* (1972): 237.

21. Wolfgang, C. "An Exploration of the Relationship Between the Cognitive Area of Reading and Selected Developmental Aspects of Children's Play." *Psychology in the Schools* 11 (1974): 338–343.

22. Kagan, J. "Reflection-Impulsivity: The Generality and Dynamics of Conceptual Tempo." *Journal of Abnormal Psychology* 71 (1966): 17–24.

23. Humphrey, J. "Comparison of the Use of Active Games and Language Workbook Exercises as Learning Media for the Development of Language Understanding with Third Grade Children." *Perceptual and Motor Skills* 21, no. 6 (1965): 23–26.

Humphrey, J. "An Exploratory Study of Active Games in Learning of Number Concepts by First Grade Boys and Girls." *Perceptual and Motor Skills* 23, no. 2 (1966): 341–342.

Zammarelli, J., and Bolton, N. "The Effects of Play on Mathematical Concept Formation." *British Journal of Educational Psychology* 47 (1977): 155–161.

24. Wallach, M. "Creativity." In *Carmichael's Manual of Child Psychology*, vol. 1, edited by P. Mussen. New York: Wiley, 1970.

Wallach, M. *The Intelligence/Creativity Distinction*. New York: General Learning Press, 1971.

Wallach, M., and Kogan, N. *Modes of Thinking in Young Children: A Study of the Creativity-Intelligence Distinction*. New York: Holt, Rinehart & Winston, 1965.

25. Ellis, M. J. *Why People Play*. Englewood Cliffs, N.J.: Prentice-Hall, 1973.

Reilly, M. *Play as Exploratory Learning*. Beverly Hills, Calif.: Sage, 1974.

26. Hutt, C. "Exploration and Play in Children." In *Play, Exploration and Territory in Mammals. Symposia of the Royal Zoological Society. op. cit.*

27. Freud, S. "Analysis of a Phobia in a Five-Year-Old Boy." In *Collected Papers*, vol. 3. London: Hogarth, 1953.

Freud, S. "Beyond the Pleasure Principle." In *The Standard Edition of the Complete Psychological Works of S. Freud, 1920–1922*, vol. 18, edited and translated by J. Strachey. London: Hogarth and the Institute of Psychoanalysis, 1955.

28. Gilmore, J. "The Role of Anxiety and Cognitive Factors in Children's Play Behavior." *Child Development* 37 (1966): 397–416.

29. Storm, B. "An Empirical Test of the Psychoanalytic Theory of Play." Unpublished master's thesis, University of Illinois, Urbana, 1977.

30. Garvey, C. *Play. op. cit.* p. 1.

CHAPTER 4

Affect As It Effects Fitness and Total Functional Integrity

Alexander W. McNeill

There remains an apparent paradox in the reasoned arguments presented by philosophers in physical education and the practice of physical education in society. The philosophers have been striving for many years to eradicate the dichotomy of the mind and the body in favor of a holistic view of the individual in which the mind and the body are interdependent.[1] Our practice, however, remains centered on skills—learning motor skills, teaching motor skills, analyzing motor skills, and, more recently, evaluating behavior evident during the performance or observation of motor skills. Skills and cognitive processes have been, and remain, the center of focus in physical education.

We have seen a considerable change in the skills being taught in physical education programs. There has been a shift from team sports and gymnastic skills to lifetime skills and outdoor activities. However, we are teaching to affect a single dimension of body phenomena, namely, the cognitive dimension. To argue that the mind and the body are not dichotomous, to identify affective as well as cognitive dimensions of body phenomena, and to suggest that these two dimensions are not discrete, does not mean that it is sufficient to influence either the cognitive or the affective component, that a suitable or proper change in the other dimension will be a necessary concomitant outcome. There being at least two dimensions to movement phenomena, it behooves physical education to address both.

In the course of the last two decades it appears that we have dissected the term "physical education," addressing the "physical" portion through teaching motor skills, taking up the "education" portion by our studies of the pedagogical sciences. We study the mechanics of the body and the changes in the systems that accompany exercise, we analyze the motor skills that constitute activity, and we examine teaching and teachers' methods and behavior.

Physical education as we know it in 1980 has been plagued by many problems during the course of its development. The physical educator is still viewed by many members of the academic community as a somewhat limited sibling. The need for academic identity and the desire to demonstrate effectiveness in the academic pursuit of knowledge have resulted in a growth pattern in physical education that focuses upon those dimensions of study traditionally considered to be academic. As a consequence physical education has been differentiated into discrete units of study such as biomechanics, motor learning, pedagogy, and exercise physiology. Each of these subunits has generated its own body of knowledge and encourages students to study a single dimension of movement phenomena, a process that results in further specialization and further differentiation. The purpose of physical education is being lost in favor of a goal or a series of goals established for one dimension of the discipline.[2]

Physical education implies something much larger than the study of movements. It implies that we may teach motor skills; it implies that we may study motor skills from various perspectives (e.g., physiological, anatomical, biomechanical, and sociological); it implies that activities and the interactions of people when they participate in activities involve the psyche as well as the body. Thus it would appear that physical education has a role in the development of the total individual.

The body concept can be defined as the impression a person has of his or her body, conscious and unconscious, affective and cognitive.[3] The concept recognizes not only the conscious cognitive aspects of body phenomena, but also the affective component of moving and being. In physical education we are just beginning to examine this affective component, but as I hope to demonstrate, this dimension may be the key to the development of physical education in the 1980's.

Physical fitness is but a part of physical education. If we view physical fitness as a product of functional integrity, then the term "physical fitness" should be considered in the same total sense as the term "physical education." Physical fitness is not just the efficient operation of various systems, but also the unmistakable, positive gestalt that is the result of the interaction of the various systems, including the psyche. Physical fitness must have the same affective and cognitive components that make up the body concept.

A primary purpose of education is to change behavior and to develop in individuals the desire to evaluate aspects of their lives rationally and make decisions about their future. Behavior may be defined as the change in states of bodies and body parts and their relationships in space.[4] Teaching specific skills may indeed establish neurological schemata that will result in the successful completion of a motor skill. That is, we have established that we are able to make a product. The question remains, What will motivate us to make that product at some time in the future?

Education is a process whereby we influence motive, establishing feelings in the individual and causing the individual to seek change actively. Motive appears to be the key to effective education.

The term "goals" may be used to imply motive. However, motive establishes goals and initiates behaviors to attain these goals. Motives can be related to feelings, and, in the case of the body, they may be feelings of pleasure or displeasure concerning its systemic functioning. Knowledge of the body as it responds to exercise, knowledge of the body as it responds to lack of exercise, knowledge of skills that will produce positive changes in systemic functioning, are all unlikely to produce a change in behavior unless a motive is established and recognized.

For a motive to be accepted it must represent the feelings of the individual seeking to change behavior. If we are to be effective in encouraging physical fitness, we must do more than just provide cognitive information; we must address the affective component of the physical fitness concept.

It was stated earlier that behavior may be defined as the change in states of bodies and body parts and their relationships in space. In physical education we study the changes in states and the relationships of bodies and body parts largely in the branch of the discipline defined as biomechanics. The changes in the systems of the body that accompany changes in position, and the accommodation or training effects that result from repetitive changes in position are evaluated in another branch of the profession defined as exercise physiology. Both branches of the profession are dependent upon the execution of motor skills.

Isaac Newton systematically observed movement and described conditions for motion that remain our basic guidelines for the physical analysis of movement. However, we might well consider that there is a parallel serious of affective "laws" or behavioral statements pertaining to human movement. These affective laws address the motive for movement. The term "motive" is used in much mechanics literature as a synonym for force; however, in modern usage it has a somewhat wider connotation.

Motive implies an inner drive, an affective condition, a feeling or series of feelings that may initiate action, accompany action, or exist after some line of action has been completed. If we were to derive a series of affective laws, we might well model them on the three classical laws proposed by Newton, addressing inertia, change in momentum, and action and reaction.

If we believe that movement and activity are necessary for total growth and development, one of our major goals must be to motivate people to participate in motor activities. Generally, healthy systemic functioning is a concomitant of participation in physical activities. Casual inspection of the activity patterns of the population suggests that we have failed to provide sufficient reasons for most people to be active. Indeed, it would appear that present, past, and future states of inactivity can be described by three affective laws. In the interest of simplicity these will be referred to as McNeill's Laws of Inactivity:

McNeill's First Law of Inactivity. A body will remain at rest, or in a uniform state of inactivity, unless it is acted upon by some internal motive.

McNeill's Second Law of Inactivity. The degree of activity or change in activity pattern is proportional to the magnitude and duration of the internal motive.

McNeill's Third Law of Inactivity. The reaction of a system stressed by exercise through the application of an internal motive is to accommodate and subsequently to supercompensate for the exercise stressor.

Regarding the first statement, inactivity is a function of lack of motive. It should be noted that motive is qualified in that it must be internally derived. Until individuals develop sufficient personal motive to participate in activity, it is unlikely that activity will result. There need be no single or best motive, merely effective motives, that is, those that result in a change in behavior from inactive to active. Changing activity patterns is like dieting to lose weight; it is not effective unless it is self-motivated and the motive results in long-term change in behavior. At present in physical education we provide knowledge of positive changes in body systems that accompany exercise, and we provide carefully planned exercise experiences with the belief that exposure will stimulate a future motive for participation. However, it has been demonstrated in other areas of health that knowledge of an adverse outcome (e.g., lung cancer) resulting from a specific behavior (e.g., cigarette smoking) is not sufficient to modify that behavior.

The second behavioral statement suggests that the degree of activity or change in activity pattern is proportional to the magnitude and the duration of the internal motive. It takes a considerable personal commitment of time and effort to harvest the benefits of a regular exercise program. It might again be emphasized that a long-term commitment to exercise as a part of normal living is the necessary prerequisite to the maintenance of a successful exercise program.

The final law is a statement of the outcomes of the application of what has come to be known as the overload principle. Essentially it implies that an internally derived motive, when used to generate a long-term exercise program, will produce a reaction that results in increased efficiency, work capacity, and recuperative abilities of the body.

To this point physical fitness activities and various exercise and training systems have not been addressed. It is not the purpose of this author to minimize the importance of these dimensions of physical education; indeed, a general overview of them is presented below. The purpose of this presentation is to establish the importance of motive, a portion of the affective dimension of activity, in the development of future goals for physical education. Physical fitness is not just a state of the body, but reflects a total functional integrity that must be defined for individuals. We must consciously address the affective dimension of movement in physical education and our fitness programs. Without internal motive, activity will remain an unlikely outcome for individuals in most Western cultures in which the machine dominates the physical working environment.

Our concept of physical fitness has undergone considerable change concomitant with the inclusion of lifetime activities in physical education programs. We have seen physical education move away from using a single concept of performance-related physical fitness in which emphasis was placed upon physiological functions to improve performance in sport and physical activities. Our concern with making athletes stronger, more skillful, faster, and more flexible is being recognized as a somewhat narrow view of fitness. More recently there has been a move to address fitness as it relates to health, in terms of both physiological and psychological functioning.[5] The profession is beginning to recognize fitness as a holistic concept rather than as a purely physical state. This position is evidenced by the development of a new Health-Related Physical Fitness Test by the Task Force on Youth Fitness of the American Alliance for Health, Physical Education, Recreation and Dance and the Physical Fitness Council of the Association for Research, Administration, Professional Councils and Societies.

The new test battery concentrates upon four basic components of fitness, namely, cardiovascular functioning, body composition, strength, and flexibility. These are some of the basic components of performance-related fitness, but the major emphasis is being placed upon cardiovascular functioning. This dimension of fitness is viewed by many physicians and health professionals as the single, most critical aspect of physical health. Regular exercise may not prevent circulatory disease, but it certainly appears to reduce the risk of severe problems, and individuals who do exercise regularly have been shown to recover more rapidly from circulatory trauma than other, less active individuals.[6] In addition, the efficient supply of oxygen to the working muscles permits prolonged work, whether for financial or recreational gain. It is readily apparent that cardiovascular efficiency, and thus cardiovascular fitness, have a great influence on our quality of life.

Body composition is addressed in the new Health-Related Physical Fitness Test battery. This dimension has been included as a result of increasing information relating obesity to coronary heart disease. Further, it has been reasoned that the increased stress of the "nonactive" workload, in the form of fat, unduly burdens the circulatory system, resulting in other problems such as hypertension, renal malfunctions, and degenerative arthritis.

Strength and flexibility for athletes are two aspects of fitness that require little explanation. However, their inclusion in the new test battery for the general population requires a little clarification. Evaluation of studies of postural defects and their relationship to chronic low back pain and acute back injuries, as well as various forms of abdominal discomfort, has led to the conclusion that weak abdominal muscles, short hamstrings, and pelvic tilt are major contributing factors to these disorders. The strength and flexibility aspects of the new test battery carefully evaluate these areas of functioning in order to identify weaknesses and recommend some corrective action before a severe disorder appears.

Although physical education has taken a giant step toward trying to influence more of the population by making the new Health-Related Physical Fitness Test more appropriate to the needs and functions of the general population, it appears that we are making the same grave error that we committed in the past. As the rationale was developed for this new test, we identified the need to address the psychological as well as the physical fitness of our people.[7] Once again we are going to evaluate cognitive and/or physical skills and levels of functioning in the hope that knowledge will provide a sufficient impetus for a change in behavior. It has been argued earlier in this chapter that knowledge cannot be integrated and molded into some form of personalized activity program until the individual exposed to that knowledge has developed some form of internal motive for participation in activity. It remains to be seen, although on the basis of past experiences we must question, whether this new test battery will generate motive for activity by making society conscious of the components of health-related fitness. This is especially true because the components of the battery are the same as some of the components of the American Alliance for Health, Physical Education, Recreation and Dance's Youth Fitness Test, despite the different emphasis.

As educators we must question the practice of evaluating the status quo in physical fitness with the belief that this knowledge will be sufficient to generate a change in behavior. For most people, reading life insurance tables of heights and appropriate weights, looking at tables predicting longevity on the basis of various health habits, and wearing seat belts to avoid injury in case of automobile accident relate to others. We all tend to identify differences in our personal lives that make these tables unsuitable for describing ourselves. It seems to be a part of modern human nature to assume that descriptive statistics relate to everyone but oneself. We might suspect that this principle will be extended to include information from our new Health-Related Physical Fitness Test battery.

In the last analysis we must return to motive and the affective component of movement. It is not sufficient to deal with the cognitive dimensions of movement and fitness. We must consciously seek to include in our physical education programs a segment that deals directly with the affective aspects of being active and improving or maintaining physical fitness. We must help in the struggle to develop internally derived motive so that goals can be identified and a beginning established toward new behaviors that include activity as a necessary part of living.

REFERENCES

1. Oberteuffer, D., and Ulrich, C. *Physical Education: A Textbook of Principles for Professional Students.* New York: Harper & Row, 1962.

2. Hoffman, S. J. "Toward a Pedagogical Kinesiology." *Quest* 28 (1977): 38–48.

3. Witkin, H. A. "Development of the Body Concept and Psychological Differentiation." In *The Body Percept,* edited by H. Werner and S. Wapner. New York: Random House, 1965.

4. Meridith, P. "The Body in the Box." Unpublished paper, Leeds University, Department of Psychology, 1965.

5. Falls, H. B. "Modern Concepts of Physical Fitness." *Journal of Physical Education and Recreation* 51, no. 4 (April 1980): 25–27.

deVries, H. A. *Physiology of Exercise for Physical Education and Athletics.* Dubuque, Iowa: Wm. C. Brown, 1980.

6. Cooper, K. H., et al. "Physical Fitness Levels vs. Selected Coronary Risk Factors: A Cross-Sectional Study." *Journal of the American Medical Association* 236 (1976): 166–169.

Frank, C. W.; Weinblatt, E.; Shapiro, S.; and Sager, R. V. "Myocardial Infarction in Men: Role of Physical Activity and Smoking in Incidence and Mortality." *Journal of the American Medical Association* 198 (1966): 1241–1245.

7. Falls, H. B. "Modern Concepts of Physical Fitness." *op. cit.*

CHAPTER 5

Curriculum Designs for Fulfilling Human Agendas

Ann E. Jewett

Curriculums in the 80's are designed for a world in turmoil. Designers are seeking to facilitate human growth and development and the capacity to adapt to potentially overwhelming environmental challenges, both physical and social in nature. Even more significant, educational leaders are looking ahead, determined to go beyond the development of survival capabilities, seeking to develop human abilities to contribute to the shaping of the future. Curriculum specialists are directing their efforts toward the shaping of curriculums designed to further the achievement of shared human goals and the fulfillment of human agendas.

Physical educators in the 80's are becoming aware of the increasingly significant role of the movement arts and sciences and of sport phenomena in creating happy, satisfying futures. They are growing more conscious of the unique potential of physical education curriculums for fulfilling human agendas. Curriculum designers have a far more difficult challenge than in the past when their role was viewed primarily as arrangement of traditional activity content into appropriate seasonal sequences and customary motor skill progressions. The identification and clarification of significant educational objectives have become functions of overriding importance. The designing of learning programs conducive to individual realization of these objectives is a continually demanding task.

Physical education in the 80's embraces an infinite number of possible curriculum designs. Designers committed to identifying the needs of individual persons in particular communities and to facilitating the search for personal meaning in movement activities are developing unique patterns. The personal curriculum of each learner is different from that of any other learner. This multitude of possible variations makes it impractical even to classify curriculum designs into categories. Rather than attempting to be all-inclusive, I offer the following descriptions of curriculums designed for the 80's.

Preschool and elementary school. Preschool education is becoming an accepted public service provided for all children during the two or three years prior to enrollment in an early childhood education program. Learning activities emphasize a combination of perceptual-motor activities, cognitive-developmental tasks, and self-care skills. Movement education activities include body-awareness and spatial-orientation challenges and games, basic motor skills, and creative movement.

All elementary school children need opportunities to participate in movement activity programs twice daily for a total of at least 40 minutes. Instructional programs include continuing movement education; ethnic, folk, and creative dance; and new games.

Much of the child's movement curriculum is organized to focus on moving in space and is designed to achieve body awareness, locomotion, object manipulation, and movement expression. Basic locomotor patterns of walking, running, sliding, and jumping are learned, adapted, and refined through imitating, experimenting, solving movement tasks set by teachers, and performing such skills in self-testing, chasing, and rhythmic games. Learning sequences progress to more complex locomotor skills such as galloping, hopping, leaping, and skipping and to advanced forms of propulsion on climbing and hanging apparatus. Students develop more sophisticated concepts of directionality and spatial relationships and better movement control through games emphasizing dodging, chasing, and tagging; through stunts, tumbling, and other gymnastic activities; through folk dance and creative dance; and through simple combatives and weight-training activities. Skating, swimming, and ethnic dances of particular local interest are recommended.

Ball- and object-handling activities involving throwing, catching, kicking, and striking receive major attention. Striking activities requiring foot-eye coordination as well as hand-eye coordination are included. Teachers plan object-manipulation challenges using hoops, ropes, wands, and batons as well as many types of balls and striking implements. Together with continuing attention to increasing efficiency in skill performance, learning sequences are designed for progressive development of strength, balance, agility, flexibility, and circulorespiratory endurance.

Elementary concepts of effective body mechanics are included. Modified track and field events are popular.

Popular games are introduced. New games and "friend" games that focus on cooperating with, assisting, and learning to know and enjoy another child are emphasized. Concepts of group interaction such as partner, team goal, sharing, win-win, teamwork, and leadership are analyzed.

Middle school. The curriculum in middle school physical education emphasizes two major elements, (a) expanded understanding of movement through refining personal skills and (b) greater depth of social understanding through experiences in movement activities of the student's own and other cultures and in creating new games. To conduct middle school education programs in developmental motor performance, each school needs the services of at least one dance educator, one aquatic specialist, and two general movement and sport educators. The dance and aquatic specialists may be shared with other middle schools in the district, depending upon enrollments. The instructional program includes survival swimming, sport skills, dance, project adventure, fitness activities, and new games. Venturesome activities requiring more personal courage are included. The concept of creating new games is appropriate to all age levels, but receives special emphasis in middle school programs. As stated by the New Games Foundation, "New Games is a process. It's not what you play . . . but how you play. This process begins with your own enjoyment, extends to an awareness of the other players, and eventually results in creating some altogether new ways to have fun." [1]

Many taped programs are available to provide for large group presentations, or for use by individual students in the learning resource center. These include innovative movement challenges and fitness-assessment activities. Audio cassettes to assist with out-of-school skill development are available for individual checkout. Instructional activities occur in three 50-minute periods weekly. Two of these provide for a planned sequential program; the third allows students to select specific activity skills, field experiences, or needed remedial work. Most students have approximately three different choices per year on a seasonal basis. The instructional program is supplemented by an intramural program directed by a full-time employee with professional career training in recreation.

Secondary school. Secondary school programs include approximately 100 hours of instruction in developmental motor performance at each level. The core course in the first year is fitness for life. It includes individual assessment of the key aspects of health-related fitness, self-monitoring of fitness achievements, guided prescription of exercise, and intensive participation in selected fitness activities. The program also includes two skill classes in which the major purpose is the development of selected movement performance skills. Selections are made by the individual student on the basis of a desire to become a competent participant or a more skilled performer.

In the second year the core course is group development through movement activities in which increased social awareness is sought; the emphasis is on cooperative games, group choreography, and community service projects. Large-group sessions featuring taped presentations of issues relating to equal opportunity in exercise, sport, and dance programs are complemented by laboratory-activity sessions in selected sport or dance forms and discussion and analysis of illustrative case studies. In addition to taking the core course, which focuses on the development of individual skills for functioning effectively in groups, each student selects two additional sport or dance skill courses.

The third and final core course emphasizes diverse approaches to seeking personal meaning in movement. Several key approaches are explored: focus on inner awareness through sport, transcendental meditation, pursuit of risk or high adventure, and the seeking of effortlessness and excellence in a particular movement form. Each student is ensured an experience in composing or creating movement and participation in a small-group wilderness-survival experience. The course concludes with a personal assessment and planning for continuing growth in developmental motor performance and life-style patterns to accommodate movement activities within a desired life-style.

Each student in the third-year program selects two additional skill classes. Over the three-year period each has completed instruction in six selected activities beyond the core courses, including at least one cooperative group game activity, one dance activity, and one outdoor activity. Each program also includes successful completion of at least one intramural season and one sport- or dance-club season.

Movement, dance, and sport is one of six core educational programs within which high school graduation requirements must be met. In addition to the core courses, three instructional units are required: Motor Development in Young Children, The Role of Exercise and Active Recreation in Aging, and International Sport and Dance. A wide variety of elective offerings in the broad field of movement, dance, and sport is available for secondary school credit.

Postsecondary education. Students enrolled in college or university or continuing education programs in physical education are required to participate in fitness-appraisal activities at least once in two years. This provides them with current fitness information and instruction in sound self-evaluation techniques, encourages personal goal setting and planning for increasing and maintaining fitness, and offers access to leisure counseling services. Higher education offerings, available at both undergraduate and graduate levels, include the following: interdisciplinary insights into effective movement to meet the demands of new occupational tasks; survival and quality living in underwater communities; exercise and fitness in limited space and in gravity-less environments; impact of popular recreational activities on the biosphere; value systems of other cultures; personal decision making to influence the shape of one's own future; consensus-seeking skills for creating quality community life; biofeedback analysis; movement notation; holography; worldwide human commonalities; senior citizens as a community resource; and urban futures planning.

GUIDELINES FOR DESIGNING
PHYSICAL EDUCATION CURRICULUMS

The preceding descriptions are broadly illustrative only. The diversity of patterns and designs appropriate for education in the 80's is infinite. Certain key commitments or directions are inherent in all sound designs, however.

The educational role of movement and sport is viewed as guidance in the search for personal meaning in movement activities. The broad range of meanings that may be sought through movement activities can be encompassed within three value clusters: fitness, performance, and transcendence. Fitness includes such standard components as strength, flexibility, and circulorespiratory endurance; yet it is specific to time-space in a changing world. Fitness is a human condition, a personal achievement involving individual understanding, self-assessment, and personal responsibility. Performance encompasses all modes of skilled motor performance in sports, dance, aquatics, gymnastics, and body mechanics activities. Persons may find meaning in skillful performance through its applications in physical recreation, job performance, survival skills, or daily functioning. Transcendence is perhaps best described as the celebration of moments of singular awareness. It is the experience of going beyond the usual, of overcoming limitations and boundaries, of personal integration and heightened consciousness of self. Movement activities offer an important channel for self-actualization and transcendence.

Sports and the movement arts are pervasive aspects of human societies around the world. The physical education curriculum of the 80's is planned with full recognition of the many roles played by the movement arts and sciences in our society, and with ample provision for educating citizens whose intention will be to modify these roles for the betterment of humankind. Because movement activities will probably continue to have significant impact on such important areas of living as health and fitness, social service, communications, leisure and recreation, and business and economics, as well as education, that impact must be positive for the society as a whole.

Physical education curriculum designers need to consider content and approaches to learning that will help us shape our future world and live happily in it. More emphasis needs to be placed on movement activities that involve us in our total environment, help to maximize a symbiotic relationship with the larger living universe, make us aware of the impact of our activities on the biosphere, and strengthen our commitment to maintain a quality environment. Global education requires opening horizons to the movement concepts and forms of other cultures. It also dictates the development of new games, especially games that de-emphasize competition and maximize cooperation. Futures education offers experiences in analyzing choices, generating alternatives, and creating movement forms and activities.

The physical education curriculum exposes learners to the total range of movement opportunities. The range is interpreted to encompass the many potential personal meanings that may be sought through movement activities, and the many alternative social roles of movement in advancing general well-being. Breadth of opportunity implies extended time and space concepts, extended forward into long-range futures, extended globally to increase experiences providing insight into other cultures.

It has long been recognized that, in any educational setting, the process may be as important as or more important than the product. Important learning outcomes in physical education include those concerned with the processes of learning to facilitate, extend, and use fully one's unique movement capabilities. Physical education curriculum designers include plans for experiencing, understanding, and gaining competence in perceiving, patterning, adapting, refining, varying, improvising, and composing in movement.

Patterns for organizing curriculum content and experiences are highly flexible. Physical education can be central in education in the 80's, but only if organizational rigidity is avoided. Only those organizational patterns are acceptable that focus on achievement of educational objectives and make learning opportunities equally accessible to all—boys and girls, persons of differing minority and ethnic backgrounds, participants of all ages, and individuals with varying degrees of motor performance skill, including the handicapped and disabled.

EDUCATIONAL COMMITMENTS IN THE 80'S

Physical education curriculum designers accept commitments common to the total academic community and strive to create programs consonant with the directions identified for shared educational futures. At least four significant commitments highlight the educational climate of the 80's in the United States:

1. The individual learner in his or her ultimate unity and personal coherence is the primary focus of the educational institution, the curriculum, and the professional staff. Curriculum planners acknowledge that a person is a holistic being, that only from a heuristic perspective can the potentials of the individual be developed to achieve personal freedom. An education designed to fulfill human agendas highlights the concepts of persons in process, of lifelong learning, and of human intentionality.

2. Ecology has become an accepted discipline and an essential component of education. Greater awareness of human oneness with the living universe is needed both to extend perceptions of self and to maintain the biosphere. Ecological validity is accessible to individual persons only as the search for a balance between humans and their environment succeeds.

3. Educational programs must be planned to develop a spirit of global community. Global education analyzes diversity and seeks to extend cultural pluralism, yet it emphasizes human commonalities. Learners are guided in developing their competency to make decisions, make judgments, and exercise influence, and in developing awareness of their involvement in the world system biologically, ecologically, socioculturally, historically, and psychologically.[2]

4. Futures education is now acknowledged to be significant curriculum content. Futurists do not agree on the shape of the future, on the specifics of the world we seek to achieve, or on the process by which we may hope to create the desired product. Most do agree, however, that human beings living in today's world will influence the shape of the long-term future. Futures education teaches students to identify critical choices, to consider and evaluate specific alternative futures, and to invent new images of the future. Most important, it opens up alternative patterns of thought for individuals and increases the possibilities of paradigm change for society. Physical education curriculum designers in the 80's share commitments to the ultimate importance of individual personal wholeness and to increased emphases on ecological education, global education, and futures education.

REFERENCES

1. New Games Foundation. *New Games Resource Catalog*. San Francisco: Author, 1979. p. i.

2. Barker, Joel A. "Three Concepts for Re-unifying K-12 Curriculum." *Futurics* 3, no. 2 (Spring 1979): 127–130.

Additional Readings

Cornish, Edward. "An Agenda for the 1980s." *The Futurist* 14, no. 1 (February 1980): 5–13.

Jewett, Ann E., and Mullan, Marie R., eds. *Curriculum Design: Purposes and Processes in Physical Education Teaching-Learning*. Washington, D.C.: American Alliance for Health, Physical Education and Recreation, 1977.

Kneer, Marian, ed. "Curriculum Theory into Practice." *Journal of Physical Education and Recreation* 49, no. 3 (March 1978): 24–37.

Nixon, John E., and Jewett, Ann E., eds. *Introduction to Physical Education*. Philadelphia: W. B. Saunders, 1980.

CHAPTER 6

Motor Skill Acquisition

Anne L. Rothstein

During the past decade, 1970-79, there has been a knowledge explosion in the processes, methods, and materials of motor skill acquisition. As with any serious explosion, this one has produced splintering and fragmenting. Splintering has come about as individuals have specialized in areas that contribute to the knowledge of motor skill acquisition and performance and have either formed their own interest groups or have limited their research and theorizing to one of the areas. Some examples of the areas are biomechanics, the principles and methods of mechanics applied to the study of the structure and function of biological systems; exercise physiology, study of the structure and function of systems underlying the physiological response to exercise; motor control, study of the factors related to the coordination and patterning of motor output; motor development, study of the age-related changes that affect the acquisition and performance of motor skills; motor learning, study of the factors related to the acquisition and performance of motor skills; sport psychology, study of the individual's behavior in sport; and sport sociology, study of group behavior in sport.

Fragmenting, which was evident before the explosion, has been exacerbated by it. "Fragmenting" describes the accumulating of the results of single studies without attempting to integrate or incorporate them into some overall pattern or design, some framework from which a picture would emerge. Study after study is conducted and the results are published with no attempt, beyond an initial review of the literature, to tie the fragments together into a meaningful whole.

If motor skill acquisition during the 1980's is to benefit from the serious but splintered and fragmented activities of the 1970's, two changes must occur. Some method or methods must be found to integrate the results of the research fragments in the various areas, and some overall framework must be used to integrate the findings from the various areas with one another and with all others. The means of accomplishing both of these are available now.[1]

Methods of integrating the results of studies from a single area have been used in other areas during the 1970's: class size;[2] special education treatment techniques;[3] neuropsychological assessment of children;[4] psychotherapy outcomes;[5] teacher "indirectness" and achievement;[6] class size and achievement;[7] and expectancy theory.[8] These methods fall under the general heading of "meta-analysis," a term coined by Glass.[9] Meta-analysis seeks to apply known methods of statistical analysis to scores derived from individual studies rather than from individual subjects. That is, the studies themselves are the experimental units for which scores are recorded. The scores are then analyzed to determine whether significant differences among the variables are common to the set of studies or to a subset of the studies. Information about these techniques is available to individuals who wish to explore them beyond the scope of this essay.[10]

The second problem, that of integrating the findings from several areas, can be accomplished by using an appropriate overall framework. During the past decade research emphasis has shifted from a product-oriented approach to a process-oriented approach.[11] In a product-oriented approach the focus is on the outcomes of experimental manipulations—for example, determining the effects of warm-up on the acquisition and performance of the volleyball serve. In a process-oriented approach the focus is on the underlying mechanisms or processes that mediate the observed change—for example, determining how and why warm-up affects acquisition and performance, not simply determining that it does. An appropriate framework for integrating the findings from the several areas of motor skill acquisition is an information-processing approach.

INFORMATION PROCESSING

Information processing explains behavior in terms of a set of sequential operations that an individual performs in attempting to be successful at acquisition or performance of motor skills. In acquisition the sequential operations would improve as learning occurred; in performance they would be executed in sequence. In the simplest explanation of information processing, these operations may be grouped into *input, decision making, output,* and *feedback.* Each of these may be further divided if a fine-grain analysis of performance is required or desired. For the purposes of this essay, however, these four will suffice.

Input encompasses those operations or processes that relate to reception of information (auditory, tactile, proprioceptive, visual) that may originate internally or externally. *Decision making* includes those processes that enable the individual to determine what the input means and what to do in response to the input. *Output* subsumes those operations that mediate response execution and control. Finally, *feedback* includes those processes that enable the performer to evaluate the just-completed performance. A simple example should serve to clarify these categories.

A softball player is at bat. The *input* includes visual information about the pitcher, the ball, the catcher, the umpire, and other players; and tactile and proprioceptive information about the weight and position of the bat, the position of the body, the convergence of the eyes, and the movement of the head. In addition, the player will have input about arousal level, fatigue state, and expectancy of success from past performance. To be successful at hitting the ball, the player must ultimately exclude all input except the speed, direction, trajectory, and spin of the ball.

Assuming that the player has, in fact, focused on the ball-flight characteristics, *decision making* consists of two aspects. First, the player must analyze and interpret the ball-flight information and determine when and where the ball will be in the striking zone (over the plate). Second, the player must choose and organize a bat-swing response that will match the predicted time and place of arrival of the ball.

Assuming that the player has interpreted the ball flight and chosen the correct response, the next step is *output.* The player must execute the response exactly as planned. This depends on the player's ability to control the systems of the body.

When the batting response has been completed, the player receives *feedback.* Information is available about whether the ball was hit, how and where it was hit, and whether the player executed the swing as planned. This information enables the player to retain successful portions of the performance and adjust or modify any aspect of the information-processing sequence judged to be ineffective.

Thus, in the information-processing sequence described above, the batter must answer four questions to hit the pitched ball successfully:

1. What is going on? (Input)

2. What does it mean? (Decision making)

3. What should I do about it? (Decision making and output)

4. What happened? (Feedback).

It should be noted that memory storage is an integral part of most information-processing models and that storage and retrieval are key concepts in the study of motor skill; however, their consideration here would needlessly complicate the presentation.

A HOLISTIC APPROACH TO MOTOR SKILL ACQUISITION

One role of the physical education practitioner is to help the learner achieve success in motor skills. Fulfilling this role requires recognition and understanding of the nature of the task to be learned and of the factors that affect the performance and the performer. It requires that the performer and the performance be viewed holistically; that is, the performance must be seen as the sum total of all the factors affecting the individual. Pertinent information may be found in the literature on biomechanics, exercise physiology, motor control, motor development, motor learning, sport psychology, and sport sociology.

Such a holistic approach is not possible at this time because of a lack of synthesis within the areas. The meta-analysis approach will be used with increasing frequency in the 1980's to synthesize information generated by studies within an area. An example of meta-analysis has been summarized by Rothstein.[12] The area of study was feedback, specifically the use of videotape replay in teaching motor skills. Three critical variables were found to be associated with the effective use of videotape replay: skill level of the performer—advanced beginners and intermediates benefited more than beginners; use of verbal cues—benefits were greater when performers were told what to look at in viewing the replay; and number of uses—performers who had multiple opportunities (five or more) to view videotape replay with interspersed practice benefited more.

Another reason for the lack of attention to the holistic approach is the lack of an overall model of skill acquisition and performance. Earlier in this chapter information processing was suggested as a possible approach. The illustration provided here uses the information-processing model and suggests ways in which the results of meta-analysis of the future might be used to clarify the teacher's role in motor skill acquisition sometime in the 1980's.

If a jigsaw puzzle on motor skills acquisition were to be created, its sections might be input, decision making, output, feedback, and memory. Within each of the sections there might be subsections on biomechanics, exercise physiology, motor control, motor development, motor learning, sport psychology, and sport sociology. Each of the sections need not include all of the subsections but only those that are relevant to the aspect under consideration. Keeping this in mind, let us take a closer look at the input section. The most prominent subsections within it are motor control, motor development, motor learning, and sport psychology. What does the information in each subsection tell the practitioner about the performer's ability to determine what is happening? A single example is provided in each case.

Motor development. There are age-related changes in a performer's ability to pick up and process input information.[13] One age-related change is the speed of visual-information processing. This may result from the development of strategies of visual search or may be the result of ignoring unimportant visual input. Regardless, the implications for the younger child are clear. If things happen too fast, the younger child is likely to miss important information. The pace of the game, of instruction, of the ball, of corrections, should be slowed to accommodate the abilities of younger children.

Motor control. As the control of movement goes from conscious to automatic, the performer is free to devote a greater percentage of attention to picking up and processing information.[14] As skill improves, the performer is required to devote less conscious attention to movement. This frees the performer to devote attention to the various sources of input information. In addition, during certain phases of movement—the beginning and the ending—greater attention to movement is required. During the middle phases of lengthy movements, then, the performer's attention is freed to monitor input. The practitioner might want to keep this in mind when planning practice. Thus he or she might shift input predictably until the performer establishes a minimum level of motor control, or might have the performer learn to monitor input, as in predicting balls and strikes in softball, without also having to plan and execute a motor response.

Motor learning. The nature of the environment (the situation in which performance takes place) can affect the performer's ability to pick up and process information.[15] Various aspects of the performance environment can affect the pickup of information: the prominence of the important input, the ratio between important and unimportant input, and the absolute number of important input items. The practitioner might wish to manipulate the performance environment to facilitate the acquisition of information (see reference number 12 for suggestions).

Sport psychology. The arousal level of the performer will affect the size of the functional visual field and, as a consequence, the performer's ability to pick up and process information.[16] As the arousal (anxiety) level of the performer increases, the visual field shrinks, effectively cutting off the performer's peripheral vision. In sports in which a wide peripheral visual field is necessary for success (e.g., soccer and basketball), the reduced field can lead to errors because important information may be outside the performer's visual field. The practitioner can assist the performer by helping reduce the stress caused by task difficulty, past failures, task danger, and unpredictability, and thus reduce arousal and increase visual-field size.

Thus, in the input phase of the information-processing sequence, factors from motor development, motor control, motor learning, and sport psychology interact to produce a unique performance. If the student succeeds, the probability is high that all went well, although a series of mistakes that cancel each other out could produce a successful performance. If the student fails, something went wrong. An important contribution of the teacher or other practitioner to skill acquisition is to assist the learner in identifying the reasons for failure and in correcting the errors. If the problem is in the input stage of the sequence, manipulating it by slowing the action, highlighting the important input, reducing the number of total input items, reducing the number of alternative events, verbally cuing the student to focus on the input rather than the movement, reducing the difficulty of the task, and reducing the uncertainty of the events, will help assure the student of success while helping him or her acquire good visual strategies. The manipulations suggested may affect performance by accommodating to (or alleviating) age-related problems, motor control difficulties of the inexperienced performer, environmentally produced difficulties, or the anxiety level of the performer. Techniques of meta-analysis will be used in identifying which of the manipulations have the greatest effect on performance, thus providing clues to the underlying process or mechanisms of input.

SUMMARY

The knowledge explosion in the motor skill area has produced splintering and fragmenting that must be controlled if physical education practitioners and learners are to benefit. This control can be achieved through synthesis using meta-analysis techniques to identify critical variables in the areas of sport sociology, sport psychology, motor learning, motor development, motor control, exercise physiology, and biomechanics. These critical variables can then be integrated using some model of motor skill acquisition and performance. The information-processing model is suggested as the most promising at present. The illustration presented demonstrates how the techniques of meta-analysis and integration might be combined during the 1980's to enhance motor skill acquisition.

REFERENCES

1. Rothstein, A. L. "Puzzling the Role of Research." *Journal of Physical Education and Recreation* 51 (1980): 39-40.

2. Cahan, L., and Filby, N. "The Class Size/Achievement Issue: New Evidence and a Research Plan." *Phi Delta Kappan* 60 (1979): 492-496.

3. Carlberg, C. *Meta-Analysis of Special Education Treatment Techniques.* Doctoral dissertation, University of Colorado, Boulder, 1979.

4. Davidson, T. B. *Meta-Analysis of the Neuropsychological Assessment of Children.* Doctoral dissertation, University of Denver, 1978.

5. Glass, G. V. "Primary, Secondary, and Meta-Analysis of Research." *Educational Researcher* 5 (1976): 3-8.

Smith, M. L., and Glass, G. V. "Meta-Analysis of Psychotherapy Outcome Studies." *American Psychologist* 32 (1977): 752-760.

6. Glass, G. V., et al. *Teacher "Indirectness" and Pupil Achievement: An Integration of Findings.* Boulder, Colo.: University of Colorado, Laboratory of Educational Research, 1977.

7. Glass, G. V., and Smith, M. L. "Meta-Analysis of Research on the Relationship of Class Size and Achievement." *Evaluation and Policy Analysis* 1 (1979): 2-16.

8. Schwab, D.; Olian-Gottlieb, J.; and Heneman, H., III. "Between Subjects Expectancy Theory Research: A Statistical Review of Studies Predicting Effort and Performance." *Psychological Bulletin* 86 (1979): 139-147.

9. Glass, G. V. "Primary, Secondary, and Meta-Analysis of Research." *op. cit.*

Glass, G. V. "Integrating Findings: The Meta-Analysis of Research." *Review of Research in Education* 5 (1977): 351-379.

10. Gage, N. L. *The Scientific Basis of the Art of Teaching.* New York: Teachers College Press, 1978.

Glass, G. V. "Primary, Secondary, and Meta-Analysis of Research." *op. cit.*

Glass, G. V. "Integrating Findings: The Meta-Analysis of Research." *op. cit.*

Rothstein, A. L. "Future Possibilities in Research Application." *Journal of Physical Education and Recreation* 51 (1980): 63-64.

11. Schmidt, R. A. "The Schema as a Solution to Some Persistent Problems in Motor Learning Theory." In *Motor Control: Issues and Trends,* edited by G. E. Stelmach. New York: Academic Press, 1976.

Stelmach, G. E. "Toward an Information-Processing Approach in Motor Behavior Research." In *Proceedings of the NAPECW/NCPEAM National Conference,* edited by L. I. Gedvilas and M. E. Kneer. Chicago: University of Illinois, 1977.

12. Rothstein, A. L. "Effective Use of Videotape Replay in Learning Motor Skills." *Journal of Physical Education and Recreation* 51 (1980): 59-60.

13. Rothstein, A. L. "Information Processing in Children's Skill Acquisition." In *Psychology of Motor Behavior and Sport II*, edited by D. M. Landers and R. W. Christina. Champaign, Ill.: Human Kinetics Publishers, 1977.

Thomas, J. R. "Acquisition of Motor Skills: Information Processing Differences Between Children and Adults." *Research Quarterly for Exercise and Sport* 51 (1980): 158–173.

14. Marteniuk, R. G. *Information Processing in Motor Skills*. New York: Holt, Rinehart & Winston, 1976.

Rothstein, A. L. "Information Processing in Children's Skill Acquisition." *op. cit.*

15. Rothstein, A. L. *An Information Processing Approach to Skill Acquisition: Perception and Timing*. 1976. ERIC Document Nos. SP 009 444; ED 111 765.

Rothstein, A. L. "Information Processing in Children's Skill Acquisition." *op. cit.*

Rothstein, A. L. "Instructional Design in Open Skills." In *Proceedings of the NAPECW/ NCPEAM National Conference*, edited by L. I. Gedvilas and M. E. Kneer. Chicago: University of Illinois, 1977.

16. Landers, D. M. "The Arousal-Performance Relationship Revisited." *Research Quarterly for Exercise and Sport* 51 (1980): 77–90.

Nideffer, R. M. *The Inner Athlete*. New York: Thomas Y. Crowell, 1976.

Rothstein, A. L. "Information Processing in Children's Skill Acquisition." *op. cit.*

Rothstein, A. L. "Instructional Design in Open Skills." *op. cit.*

CHAPTER 7

The S/*: The Transcendent
Experience in Sport

Virginia Martens Hayes

Many sport sociologists maintain that sport represents a microcosm of its culture because it reflects the patterns of the larger society. Increased public intrigue with transcendental phenomena strongly supports this idea and has unearthed some fascinating material on the transcendental experience in sport.

Public interest in the human potential movement has grown steadily since the mid-1950's and early 1960's. Factors including the impact of World War II, fear of nuclear weapons, technological alienation, fear of social computerization, the civil rights and women's movements, and the counterculture of the 1960's have undoubtedly contributed to the development of the human potential movement. Major social institutions such as education, business, medicine, and sport have all been affected, and meditation, yoga, self-actualization, and transcendence are no longer foreign concepts. Although the offshoots of the human potential movement are quite diverse, germane to each of them is an increased focus on the individual realizing his or her potential.

Many academicians, philosophers, and scientists believe that the human quest to transcend self is inherent in human nature and that the desire to alter consciousness periodically is an innate drive similar to the hunger or sexual drive.[1] History reinforces this idea, for reports of transcendence and altered states of consciousness are present in virtually every culture.[2] The transcendent experience is certainly not a new phenomenon. Recently several explanations of it have been offered: (a) the experience aids in species survival because spontaneous visionary moments have enhanced the viability of the individual in society; (b) the experience is accidental and without meaning, analogous to a short circuit in an electrical wiring system; and (c) the experience is one of receiving those elements subsumed under the word "God."[3]

This essay will focus on the transcendental experience in sport, which includes any extraordinary perceptual experience in the sport environment. First, however, the essay will look at the broader cultural context in which this sport phenomenon occurs.

Historically, studies of human transcendent experiences have been severely hampered by cultural restrictions. Because the experience was considered highly sacred, church officials believed that critical analysis would destroy its religious power and render its meaning insignificant. Consequently it was not actively investigated. The transcendent experience also has occurred in secular settings. Unfortunately the scientific community has ignored the phenomenon, considering it pathological, ridiculous, and unworthy of scientific scrutiny because of its subjective nature. Only in the current cultural climate has the public, intrigued by the human potential movement, requested information on the human capacity for transcending ordinary states of consciousness.

Examining the transcendent phenomenon, however, encounters several distinct problems: (a) because a transcendent experience is communicated subjectively, personal interpretation and fluency of communication seriously affect standardization. Subtle differences in language, terminology, metaphor, and meaning also contribute to potential misinterpretations of subjective reports. (b) Because cultural logic, language, and taboos determine an individual's perception of the experience, establishing any conviction with scientific certainty is difficult. (c) Because a transcendent experience may require a deterioration of reasoning and observational abilities, validity and measurement pose real problems for investigators. The experience also cannot be validated empirically. (d) Because the transcendent experience is complex and varied, the scientific method of inquiry may not be able to explain it fully.

Consequently, even though the transcendent experience has existed for thousands of years, very little is actually known about it. In sport, little research has been directed toward the individual's subjective experience and the possibilities for realizing full potential. Problems of measurement, lack of a common language, and pragmatic concerns about improving sport performance have all hampered research efforts. Although the number of studies about the human potential movement in relation to sport is slowly increasing, little research exists on altered states of consciousness in sport.

Crystallized from the author's master's thesis, this essay will synthesize and analyze the available literature on the transcendent experience in sport from theoretical insights and subjective reports. The transcendent experience in sport will be referred to hereafter as the S/*. This symbol is a synthesis of elements common to various interpretations of the transcendent experience in sport and was created to illustrate the human's relationship to the experience. As William James succinctly wrote:

> One conclusion was forced upon my mind at that time, and my impression of its truth has ever since remained unshaken. It is that our normal waking consciousness, rational consciousness as we call it, is but one special type of consciousness, whilst all about it, parted from it by the filmiest of screens, there lie potential forms of consciousness entirely different. We may go through life without suspecting their existence; but apply the requisite stimulus, and at a touch they are there in all their completeness, definite types of mentality which probably somewhere have their field of application and adaptation.[4]

The solidus (/) is the filmy screen which James refers to, also the wall suggested by Huxley,[5] the curtain of C. S. Lewis,[6] and the culturally determined boundaries of an individual's perceptual reality. The "S" represents the sport environment. The star (*) is the stellar moment that can grace an individual if the screen is penetrated. The fragile yet potent and rare qualities of the experience are also symbolized by the star. In addition, the star serves as a fitting reminder of the relativity of human perceptions: from one perspective a star may seem like a speck of light in a black-velvet sky; from a different view a star can assume immense importance as giver of light, heat, and life. Although the S/* is but a pinprick in the vast tapestry of human experience, its impact and significance can encompass dimensions of infinite magnitude.

Terms in the literature on sport that have been used to describe the S/* are: "perfect moment," "peak-experience in sport," "flow experience," and "greatest moment in sport." Although the term "perfect moment" originated in Sartre's novel *Nausea*, Carolyn Thomas has written most extensively on it in relation to sport. In her dissertation, *The Perfect Moment: A Sport Aesthetic*,[7] she maintained that the perfect moment can very nearly be equated with Maslow's concept of the peak-experience[8] in terms of intensity and affective involvement.

Maslow created the term "peak-experience" around 1956. Other authors[9] have contributed extensively to a broader understanding of the concept.

Mihalyi Csikszentmihalyi [10] created the term "flow experience" in the early 70's to characterize a nonordinary experience in which awareness merges with action into a state of oneness.

Many authors [11] have used the phrase "greatest moment in sport" to describe the S/*. It is an umbrella term that encompasses the S/* as well as other experiences such as moments of immense pride after a victory. Its exact origins are therefore imprecise.

In the literature on sport it is significant that these terms describing the S/* are used synonymously. Csikszentmihalyi [12] noted that the flow experience was analogous to experiences that have usually been called transcendent or religious, and he cited the religious experience and Maslow's peak-experience as closely related to the flow experience. Thomas [13] also observed the similarities between the perfect moment and Maslow's peak-experience. Other authors [14] have similarly used the "greatest moment in sport" and the "peak-experience in sport" to describe the S/*.

To determine whether writers on sport were discussing the same phenomenon but using different vocabulary, this author analyzed the emotional, perceptual, psychological, and spiritual elements of the perfect moment, peak-experience in sport, flow experience, and greatest moment in sport. The elements were then compared and synthesized to describe the S/*. In the emotional category spontaneity, intensity, and an emotional continuum were suggested. The literature supported the idea that the individual was powerless to evoke the S/* or affect its duration. The experience was also considered highly intense, and although emotional reactions ranged from calm to joy, a continuum would account for individual differences.

In the perceptual category increased awareness during the S/* was the first characteristic. This awareness was not solely rational, but involved more of a total body knowing. Second, the ego was transcended and the S/* was perceived as unique, nonordinary, and demanding the individual's undivided attention in the present moment. Finally, the experience was considered an end in itself and not a means to an end.

Under the psychological category the integration of body, mind, and spirit, the notion of total species acting, was pervasive throughout the literature. A second concept was the idea of the individual's being at the peak of power and fully functioning during the S/*. A third characteristic was the passive/active interaction that occurred during the S/*; although the individual was powerless to evoke the S/*, it did require total commitment to the activity.

Under the spiritual category union with a greater presence was suggested.

Definitions of the four experiences that dealt with altered perception in sport were also analyzed and synthesized into an acceptable definition of the S/*: the S/* represents a spontaneous, unique, nonutilitarian experience in the sport environment occurring with different intensities, in which a skilled and totally committed individual merges with an Other. "Spontaneous" refers to the unexpected nature of the experience. "Unique" and "nonutilitarian" suggest that the experience is extraordinary and is considered an end in itself. The experience occurs within a sport environment and has different degrees of intensity. "Skilled" suggests that the individual has attained sufficient expertise to forget himself or herself in the experience. "Totally committed" refers to the maximum commitment from the individual, and "merges with an Other" suggests that the individual may be psychologically integrated, unified with the environment, or merging with a greater power during the experience.

The author also analyzed environmental conditions prior and during the S/*. From the available literature the occurrence of the S/* does not appear to be limited to certain sport environments. Reports of the S/* occurred most frequently in publications on jogging, running, mountain climbing, parachuting, skiing, and surfing. Although factors inherent in these sports may be responsible for the greater number of S/* reports, it is also quite possible that little information has been published on other less well known sports that have equal or greater potential for evoking the S/*. Factors such as public interest in a particular sport; public receptivity to transcendent experiences; motivation and willingness of sport participants to share experiences of altered consciousness; and verbal and literary proficiency of sport participants to communicate the experience may determine how much available literature exists on a particular sport.

Many authors have noted that the sport environment is particularly conducive to the occurrence of altered states of consciousness. Detached from the ordinary world, the sport environment provides the individual with complete freedom. Thomas[15] noted that sport is a nonordinary, nonutilitarian reality operating according to its own set of predetermined rules. As such it has a definite beginning and end and provides opportunities for intense involvement and individual insight. This freedom to act without utilitarian motives enables individuals to commit themselves totally to the experience. This total commitment is a necessary precondition to the S/*.

Other characteristics of sport may also make it an environment conducive to the occurrence of the S/*. Discipline is necessary for excellence in sport; perhaps this frees the mind to experience the S/*. Csikszentmihalyi[16] also noted that sport provides opportunities for absorption, narrowing of focus of awareness, loss of self-consciousness, responsiveness to clear goals, unambiguous feedback, and a sense of control over the environment. These may enable a S/* to occur more readily than in other arenas such as literature or music.

The author also investigated the relationship between a sport environment and the occurrence of the S/*. Reports of the S/* were not limited to a certain sport environment. Factors such as rhythm and repetition, swift movement, eustress, increased elevation, exhaustion, pain, and fear occurred frequently in the literature and may provide clues about sport environments that are conducive to the S/*.

Jogging and rhythmical sport activities were frequent backgrounds in which the S/* occurred. Several authors[17] have suggested that the rhythmicity and repetition act as a mechanism that tires and frustrates the rational mind—much like a mantra, koan, or focus on breathing. Once the controlling mechanism is out of the way, altered states of consciousness may more readily occur. Kostrubala[18] has also linked the repetition in running to neurophysiological research. He has hypothesized that the running rhythm wears out the dominant, logical, sequentially ordered left side of the brain, and this allows the right side of the brain, which is essentially intuitive, aesthetic, creative, nonlogical, and nonsequential, to break into consciousness.

Sports in which swift movement occurs have also been suggested as conducive to the S/*. Laski[19] found that swift movement was a common trigger for ecstasy, and skiing, flying, driving in a fast car, skating, or sky diving were frequently mentioned in connection with the S/*.

The concept of eustress was connected often with the S/*. Furlong[20] suggested that high-risk sports may trigger a unique level of elation in humans and that the most difficult and dangerous sports aroused the highest feelings. Sports such as skiing, surfing, sky diving, horseback riding, and hang gliding all contain elements of risk and speed; it was not clear whether the pleasurable stress of the risk activity, its speed and swift movement, or a combination of elements evoked the S/*. Furlong believed that a chemical might account for the unusual elation after certain risk sports; current research on endorphins may intimately tie in with this theory. In addition, Furlong believed that individuals must take risks within their own competence to achieve the S/*. His research indicated that novices rarely if ever achieved the euphoria of risk-exercise because they were petrified.

Mountain climbing was also frequently mentioned as a sport in which the S/* occurred. Perhaps alterations in elevation and levels of oxygen represent other contributing factors to the S/*.

In the sport literature, rhythm and repetition, swift movement, eustress, and increased elevation appear to be significant factors in determining whether or not a S/* occurred. However, numerous accounts of the S/* also exist in sports such as basketball, tennis, sailing, and gymnastics. Exhaustion, fear, and pain may also contribute to the occurrence of the S/*. Although other unknown factors undoubtedly exist, perhaps the extreme concentration and subsequent exhaustion and relaxation occurring in many sports trigger the S/*.

The sport environment, therefore, appears to be highly significant for the occurrence of the S/*. Although all sports have the potential for at least one of the factors cited above, perhaps sports characterized by several factors are more conducive to the occurrence of the S/* than sports characterized by only one factor.

In the literature on sport the S/* occurs in both competitive and noncompetitive environments. Lack of information on the S/* makes it difficult to assess whether the S/* is a common occurrence in a sport population. Ravizza [21] found that nearly all of the athletes whom he spoke with could recall a unique S/* that had occurred in their lives. Among other factors, fear of ridicule, public uneasiness with reports of altered states of consciousness, lack of a descriptive language, and varying abilities and desires to verbalize the S/* have severely affected the amount of available literature on the S/*. It may be a more common experience than the limited evidence suggests.

In an individual's lifetime the S/* is a relatively rare phenomenon. Subjective reports of the S/* ranged in frequency from zero to (most commonly) one or two to dozens. Perhaps the dozens were less intense than the more cataclysmic one or two most commonly reported. Evidence on duration also ranged from a momentary experience to days of "being in the groove" to a whole season. Most commonly the S/* lasted only for moments or for part of a game.

The literature also suggests that the S/* may occur to an individual alone or with others. It has seemed to occur most often when the individual has been alone, but evidence indicates that it can be shared to a certain extent by several individuals or fostered in other members of a team.

Very little information is available on whether the S/* can be induced. Spino [22] has suggested that there is no absolute way of predicting when altered states of consciousness may appear. Some happen after sustained diligence and others occur quite by chance. Kostrubala,[23] Fixx,[24] Spino,[25] and Reich [26] have offered schemes to induce the S/*. Spino and Hickman's theories [27] are interesting from a biochemical framework. Recent scientific discoveries have shown that the most inhibiting factor in muscular activity is the production of lactic acid in the blood. When the supply of oxygen is inadequate, lactic acid escapes from the muscles into the bloodstream. Because ten minutes of meditation can reduce the lactic acid level in the blood to the same degree as eight hours of sleep, perhaps breakthroughs in sport will occur when the individual learns how to reduce the lactic acid in the blood.[28] Meditation, hypnosis, autogenic training, and biofeedback may help an individual develop a passive type of concentration that is necessary to become completely immersed in an activity. In the future they may provide keys to unlock the secrets of the mind-state most conductive to the S/*.

After considering the external environmental conditions of the S/*, the author investigated individuals' perceptions before and during the S/*. Categorizing physical, mental, emotional, social, and spiritual aspects was useful in isolating pertinent relationships to the S/*. These categories form arbitrary divisions and blend together like colors in a spectrum. Although certain facets of internal perception fall under a particular category, they should be placed in the context of the whole person functioning.

In many cases, before and during the S/* the individual was moving. An increase in sensitivity and bodily perception was also noted, as well as effortlessness and complete control during the S/*. The individual felt powerful and strong and experienced increased coordination during the perfection of the intense S/*. "Lightness," "grace," "fluidity," and "a floating feeling" were frequently used to describe the S/*.

In the category of mental perception many athletes noted heightened awareness during the S/*. This heightened level of perception was so acute that individuals focused exclusively on the immediate moment and became totally absorbed in the activity. Many athletes also noted the extreme clarity that accompanied this intense awareness. Others reported they felt extreme confidence, power, and control yet lack of control; a wiser intuitive knowing that transcended intellectualization or rational thought guided their actions. Loss of self-consciousness, loss of ego, self-transcendence, and self-forgetfulness were also frequently reported during the S/*. The loss of self-consciousness was accompanied by a union with the environment in which the individual was no longer in control of, but was controlled by, the activity. This situation is paradoxical because through loss of control, the individual actually gained more control. Also, athletes noted time and space disorientation and loss of fear during the S/*.

Through the literature on sport, authors have suggested conditions that facilitate the S/*. Many of these ideas are interrelated and cluster around the concepts of letting go, mastery of technique, positive attitude and self-image, concentration, awareness in the present, total commitment, and intention.

Emotional reactions to the S/* ranged from joy, awe, wonder, satisfaction, exhilaration, excitement, and elation, to humbleness and calm. Expressions of wonder, exhilaration, awe, and joy were more evident in the literature than were expressions of calm, humbleness, and placidity. The S/* undoubtedly varies in intensity among individuals. This may explain the continuum of emotional responses encountered. As noted earlier, evidence also suggests that the S/* occurs when the individual is either alone or in a group, although it occurs more often in solitude.

Under spiritual perception, many athletes noted their awareness of the presence of life forces greater than themselves; the idea of union and of merging with something greater was cited frequently in the literature. Reports of total harmony, union, perfection, oneness, wholeness, integration, and fusion occurred often. This integration could occur on several levels (e.g., union of mind, body, and spirit; union of human with environment; and union of human with a greater presence), but the S/* was often described as sacred. Although they did not usually use religious terms, athletes implied that the S/* was the greatest moment in their life—a perfect, correct, and complete experience. Another recurrent spiritual concept was the idea of passivity and surrender to something greater, enabling individuals to transcend their usual performance in sport. Despite largely nonreligious interpretations of the S/*, from the common qualities of union, letting go, and passivity/activity and from descriptions of its impact and meaning, the S/* appears to contain deeper spiritual elements that are not influenced by local dogma or doctrine.

Analysis of the literature on sport suggests that the S/* is a phenomenon in which the total individual is the best he or she can be in this world. The S/* represents perfect integrated action of the individual who accepts his or her limitations and celebrates the freedom and joy this provides. Because the study of the S/* is in its infancy, increased social interest will generate much-needed information about this phenomenon.

Interdisciplinary research is crucial because of the complexity of the S/*. Ideas from transpersonal education including visual imagery, fantasy, and concentration exercises may build bridges to the enticing realm of the S/*. Research on left- and right-hemisphere brain activity, oxygen depletion, lactic acid control, adrenalin increase, eustress, meditation, and endorphins may also contribute significantly to understanding the phenomenon. Complicated interrelationships undoubtedly exist among genetic predispositions, personality characteristics, attention span, stress, tolerance, skill, and the omnipresent mystery factor(s); equations may be developed in the future to help us interpret the importance of these factors.

The path toward understanding is steep, winding, and fraught with enticing detours. It is therefore essential that psychological, sociological, political, and historical factors be integrated with biochemical explanations to provide a meaningful context in which to interpret the S/*.

REFERENCES

1. Rosenfeld, E. *The Book of Highs: 250 Methods for Altering Your Consciousness Without Drugs*. New York: New York Times Book Co., 1973.

Greeley, A. *Ecstasy: A Way of Knowing*. Englewood Cliffs, N.J.: Prentice-Hall, 1974.

Weil, A. *The Natural Mind: A New Way of Looking at Drugs and Higher Consciousness*. Boston: Houghton Mifflin, 1972.

2. Watts, A. "This Is It." In *The Highest State of Consciousness*, edited by J. White. New York: Doubleday, 1972.

3. Cohen, S. *The Beyond Within: The LSD Story*. New York: Atheneum, 1965.

4. James, W. *The Varieties of Religious Experience*. New York: Random House, 1902. p. 298.

5. Huxley, A. *The Doors of Perception and Heaven and Hell*. New York: Harper & Row, 1954.

6. Lewis, C. S. *Surprised by Joy*. New York: Harcourt, Brace, 1955.

7. Thomas, C. *The Perfect Moment: A Sport Aesthetic*. Unpublished doctoral dissertation, The Ohio State University, 1972.

8. Maslow, A. *Toward a Psychology of Being*. New York: Van Nostrand Reinhold, 1962.

9. Ravizza, K. *A Study of the Peak Experience in Sport*. Unpublished doctoral dissertation, University of Southern California, 1973.

Ravizza, K. "Potential of the Sport Experience." In *Being Human in Sport*, edited by D. J. Allen and B. W. Fahey. Philadelphia: Lea & Febiger, 1977.

Houts, J. "Feeling and Perception in the Sport Experience." *Journal of Health, Physical Education and Recreation* 41 (October 1970): 71–72.

Gallwey, T. *Inner Tennis: Playing the Game*. New York: Random House, 1976.

10. Csikszentmihalyi, M. *Beyond Boredom and Anxiety: The Experience of Play and Work in Games*. Chicago: Jossey-Bass, 1976.

11. White, D. A. "Great Moments in Sport: The One and the Many." *Journal of the Philosophy of Sport* 2 (1975): 124–32.

Nideffer, R. M. *The Inner Athlete: Mind plus Muscle for Winning*. New York: Thomas Y. Crowell, 1976.

Kostrubala, T. *The Joy of Running*. Philadelphia: J. B. Lippincott, 1976.

12. Csikszentmihalyi, M. *Beyond Boredom and Anxiety: The Experience of Play and Work in Games*. op. cit.

13. Thomas, C. *The Perfect Moment: A Sport Aesthetic*. op. cit.

14. Gallwey, T. *Inner Tennis: Playing the Game*. op. cit.

Murphy, M., and Brodie, J. "I Experience a Kind of Clarity." *Intellectual Digest* 3, no. 5 (January 1973): 19–22.

15. Thomas, C. *The Perfect Moment: A Sport Aesthetic*. op. cit.

16. Csikszentmihalyi, M. *Beyond Boredom and Anxiety: The Experience of Play and Work in Games*. op. cit.

17. Kostrubala, T. *The Joy of Running. op. cit.*

Spino, M. *Beyond Jogging: The Inner Space of Running.* Millbrae, Calif.: Celestial Arts, 1976.

Maslow, A. *Toward a Psychology of Being. op. cit.*

18. Kostrubala, T. *The Joy of Running. op. cit.*

19. Laski, M. *Ecstasy: A Study of Some Secular and Religious Experiences.* New York: Greenwood Press, 1961.

20. Furlong, W. "Danger as a Way of Life." *Sports Illustrated* 30: (January 27, 1969): 52–53.

21. Ravizza, K. "Potential of the Sport Experience." *op. cit.*

22. Spino, M. *Beyond Jogging: The Inner Space of Running. op. cit.*

23. Kostrubala, T. *The Joy of Running. op. cit.*

24. Fixx, J. F. "Runners Really Are Different." *Running: The Magazine for Thinking Runners* 3, no. 1 (1978): 5–13.

25. Spino, M. *Running Home.* Millbrae, Calif.: Celestial Arts, 1977.

26. Reich, L. "Try Not to Think About It." *Runner's World Magazine* 9, no. 2 (February 1974): 17.

27. Spino, M., and Hickman, J. L. "Beyond the Physical Limits." *Runner's World Magazine* 12, no. 3 (March 1977): 52–53.

28. Spino, M. *Beyond Jogging: The Inner Space of Running. op. cit.*

Additional Readings

Allen, D. J., and Fahey, B. W. *Being Human in Sport.* Philadelphia: Lea & Febiger, 1977.

Thomas, C. "Toward an Experiential Sport Aesthetic." *Journal of the Philosophy of Sport* 1 (September 1974): 67–91.

White, J., ed. *The Highest State of Consciousness.* New York: Doubleday, 1972.

CHAPTER 8

Sanity in Sport

Celeste Ulrich
LeRoy T. Walker

Amateur athletics in the United States has a unique pattern of organization. It is unlike that of any other country in the world. It uses physical education curriculums as its training program and has avoided rigid centralization of authority. Consequently, amateur athletics in the United States has a variety of patterns, all of which have both assets and liabilities.

For the majority of children the first major introduction to the organized athletic world comes through participation on a school team or in a school event that uses the skills taught in physical education classes. Most of the activities taught in physical education classes use sport, aquatics, gymnastics, and dance as their modus operandi, and the acquisition of performance skills is the core concern of the majority of physical education classes. Beginning skills for sport are usually introduced sometime about the fourth grade and are refined and expanded upon throughout the remaining school years.

As the skills are acquired, the individual learns to use them in performance situations that are set up for public demonstration. Thus the physical education student may slowly become the athlete, the gymnast, the swimmer, the dancer.

Like the role of the participant, the role of the teacher of physical education also may begin to mutate. As the teacher guides highly skilled students into public performance opportunities, the teacher becomes the coach. Although there are certain aspects of teaching and coaching that are congruent and even synonymous, the two roles are distinct from each other and at times not mutually supportive.

The teacher's obligation is to make sure that each student has an equal opportunity to learn and that all students are treated equitably. Often the teacher tends to help the poorer student to achieve, sometimes with the result that the better student progresses on a self-initiated and -monitored program. The teacher is especially concerned about self-actualization for all students, including the atypical ones, and emphasizes adaptive techniques that aid self-discovery. The good teacher uses many evaluation techniques that are attentive to cognitive, affective, and motoric behaviors and that assist the student in knowing when to take the next step. The teacher's relationship with the student is often a warm and caring one, but it is seldom an intimate one. Instead, the teacher depends heavily upon interaction techniques that insist that the student arrive at the threshold of self-discovery and self-actualization. Self-discovery is very sensitive to individual differences and places only minimal importance on the ability of the student to act in concert with other members of the class, except in a few specially structured situations.

In contrast, the coach has the obligation to identify those participants who are capable of outstanding contributions and to hone their abilities to a fine and sharp edge. Although there is no deliberate effort to isolate the most highly skilled from the skilled, the very process of selection for public performance ensures a pattern that facilitates the emergence of the apt and decrees that average performers be served in other ways. Athletics is organized to be exclusive. The coach does not hesitate to choose the best and to allow the best to excel. Indeed, the coach's job is to develop individual excellence.

Because the opportunity for peak performance is usually concentrated in a game, a meet, or a recital, the time element for preparation does not easily cater to self-discovery and self-actualization methodology. The coach is considered an exemplary model of knowing. Techniques are mastered in the manner prescribed by the coach. Strategy and performance patterns are devised by the coach and executed according to the coach's plan. Not only is the game plan, the performance pattern, or the choreography interpreted by the coach; it is often devised by the coach. The coach is especially concerned with weaving together an integrated and coordinated performance that, while allowing individuals to star, is attentive to strong support patterns from the nonstars. As long as the eventual success of the public performance is in doubt, the coach has no qualms about using a few selected individuals who will contribute to total success.

For the most part, the most significant evaluation of the coach's endeavor is the public judgment accorded the performance; the win, the beautiful concert, are both criteria for coaching evaluation. The participants measure their success by the public's comments and individual or coach appraisal. If there is some spin-off in terms of self-discovery, self-actualization, and individual satisfaction, the coach is pleased and richer in feelings of self-worth, but such spin-off is not essential to the coach's task.

The coach's relationship with the individual performer and the team or troupe is an intimate one. It is not unusual for the coach to play the role of the surrogate parent, the big brother or sister, the personal confidante, the guidance counselor. The performance of the potential star is seen by the coach as a truly integrated experience. The coach feels very responsible to attend to the whole person because any one facet of a performer's life-style may have a serious effect upon his or her performance. Coaches are usually sensitive people and play a multitude of interacting roles. Each role is calculated to help the athlete or performer reach the zenith of individual skill.

Just as teachers differ from coaches, so students differ from athletes. The student is concerned with the acquisition of knowledge and usually expects to have an important role in his or her education. For the student the class is a time to seek sympathetic and sensitive evaluation with the hope that the teacher will be alert to and thoughtful about past knowledge and experiences. Ordinarily students expect teachers to be understanding rather than demanding, and hope that their efforts as students (no matter what the quality) will be ameliorated by the teacher's insights, concerns, and obligations to education.

The athlete, on the other hand, usually hopes to be trained. The expectation is that the coach will be concerned with improving specific performance patterns rather than educating. The performer desires that the short time the coach has with him or her be spent in refining skill and movement forms through expert analysis rather than through more laborious and esoteric self-discovery techniques. Most athletes hope that their coach will be demanding (albeit sensitively so) and usually have a great respect for the taskmaster. Athletes want their coach to see them as whole performers and hope for comradeship with the coach and the team, a comradeship that is satisfying and personal. The athlete may expect a certain amount of personal privilege in terms of preparation for performance, but usually is more concerned with the total endeavor than with self. Many athletes are astute performance evaluators and are even willing not to participate if they are convinced that their performance would be deleterious to the total effort. To "ride the boards" is no disgrace, nor does it suggest that one's performance potential does not have value.

As the student is different from the athlete and the teacher is different from the coach, so the class is different from the game/performance. The class is structured to reveal new understandings and new patterns of synthesis. The class is structured to permit an interacting format that can accommodate tangential knowledge as well as that which was the anticipated focus. The class's atmosphere is planned to ensure comfort and ease and to reduce tensions. There is usually a friendly pattern of action that is supportive of each member and that reduces conflict as quickly as possible. The end result of the class is measured in the ability of the teacher and the student to be commonly attentive to a subject, with the teacher responsible for structuring the class format and the student responsible for altering the format to answer individual needs, natures, and desires.

The game and performance are planned to demonstrate the logic and insights of the athletes and their coach. The public performance is pinpointed on success that has a measurable component. The performance usually generates tension, and although various patterns are used to reduce some of the tension, the generally accepted understanding is that athletes/performers should be "keen," "on edge," and "hungry." The arena of the contest is usually one of controlled competition. Sometimes the competition is with self, sometimes with the performance of others, and at still other times with standards of excellence that have already been demonstrated by past performers or that are thought possible by virtue of empirical observations. The end result of the game/performance is measured in how close the coach and the athlete are able to come to a commonly acceptable goal of excellence. Both the athlete and the coach have to "feel good" about the result in an honest bilateral appraisal of the performance. The carefully orchestrated performance contains the seeds of exaltation and remonstration, both of which may be felt intensely because of the public's expectations. Attention is always paid in the game/performance to the quality of the demonstration, and there is special sensitivity to third-party evaluation.

Because the public performance with the coached participant is markedly different from the contained class with the self-actualized, educated student, it is difficult for people who play dual roles as student and athlete or teacher and coach to discern exactly which role is being played and when one is more cogent than the other. Although there are numerous overlaps in the role-playing opportunities, as indeed there are overlaps in the class/public performance situation, the subtle differences sponsored by each of the situations foster ambivalence and at times confusion.

It is into this confused pattern that physical education and athletics are often cast. For many years there was a concerted attempt to blend the symbiotic roles and situations and to insist that they were indeed essentially the same. Combining athletics and physical education administratively was a desirable pattern. Facilities and equipment could be shared, personnel could assume both teacher and coach roles, financial resources could be shared, and some desirable restraint could be exacted from athletics even as education basked in honest attention to the gifted. It looked as if the joint arrangement could (and certainly should) be reasonable and desirable. There were many who believed that an athletic program should be the outcome of a good physical education program.

Such a joint plan for administering physical education and athletics was initiated on a wide scale in the early part of the twentieth century and continues in many places today. The combination is usually found in the junior high, intermediate, and secondary schools of the country and is also found, to some extent, in small colleges and universities and junior and community colleges. Until a decade ago the joint administrative format was found in all physical education and athletic opportunities offered to females, no matter what the educational level.

Slowly the administrative combination of physical education and athletics is being changed. The change is occurring because of the emphasis upon the development of the world-class athlete and upon the employment of the recruiter-coach. The change is further intensified because many institutions of education have recognized the public relations possibilities of athletics. Thus, in the 80's the organization and administration of physical education and athletics is evolving to reflect the perceived differences between the coach/athlete/game and the teacher/student/class.

The administrative change has brought both assets and liabilities to programs of physical education. What was thought might be a commonly acceptable pattern of cooperation has often deteriorated into conflictual styles and power plays. The common need for facilities and equipment is being resolved by identifying special facilities and purchasing special equipment for athletics. The varsity field, the Olympic pool, the theatre stage, are being reserved for the gifted performers who are products of the coaching process. "Game balls" and special bats, clubs, sticks, and rackets are being designated for the athlete/performer who needs finely tuned instruments. There is the general understanding that physical education classes do not use athletic equipment and facilities because such use would render them unfit for the more highly skilled performers. The public performance is often dependent upon the sensitivity of both the facility and the equipment. In addition, it seems essential to ensure that time be allotted to the development of superior performance. As the recreational and extracurricular opportunities for those who want additional experience threaten to usurp the training time of the coach who is attempting to develop the best public performance possible, there occurs a struggle between physical educators and coaches as to who will be given the available facility, at what time, and for how long.

Because the development of the athlete insists upon display and because it has become increasingly important for the school to produce successful athletic performances, emphasis is now being put upon the public relations potential of the game/performance. Success depends not only on the coaches' ability but also on the availability of the prospective athlete, so it seems important to many coaches to recruit potential athletes for their institution. Such recruiting is conducted to ensure a successful performance in the eyes of the general public. Thus the coach has become responsible for recruiting in addition to the already prescribed job of training. Recruiting has insisted that lures be established to attract athletes to specific situations. The legal lures have been the opportunity to be associated with a winning team, to be coached by a special individual, to be scouted for professional play, and to get some financial help with one's education. The illegal lures—material products, money, special privileges—are increasingly difficult to control because they are often offered by people outside the educational establishment, including merchants, alumni and alumnae, and fans.

Because athletics is expensive, a great deal of money is needed to sponsor it. Departments of physical education hesitate to use a disproportionate share of their budget on an experience that benefits only a few elite participants, and the general public continues to be leery of the use of tax money for what is judged to be quasi-educational. Many states have passed laws ensuring that tax money cannot be used to fund athletics. It has become apparent that money must be collected to support athletics from sources that are not earmarked for education.

As a result of the absence of funds, those who are concerned with the continuing development of athletics have sought money from nontraditional sources. Admission is charged to attend a performance; gifts are solicited from the community to help pay for uniforms and equipment; covert patterns of support are instigated in the form of maintenance, administration, and salaries; and the earning power of the athlete is organized to facilitate payments by the media and revenue sharing in championships. Athletics is big business. In many instances it can no longer be contained in the department of physical education. Both physical education and athletics are squirming to find different administrative and organizational patterns.

For a number of years the separation of the two ventures seemed like the logistically logical solution. Such separation, however, posed some philosophic problems. Could athletics maintain an educational aura if it moved outside the traditional educational pattern of the disciplines? Could the rather expensive physical education program be funded without some revenue production? Would there continue to be administrative problems with facilities, equipment, personnel, and scheduling?

With some apprehension it has been agreed in many instances that a department of athletics should be given a chance. Starting in the colleges and universities, athletics has begun to sever itself from physical education. In the beginning some of the athletic directors were former physical educators, and many of the coaches had their roots in the teaching of skill in physical education classes. However, these patterns are changing; in increasing instances former athletes are being hired for both administrative and coaching positions. The theory is that performers should be successful at administering an enterprise in whose design they had excelled. In some cases the athletics-physical education split has been amicable. In a significant number of other cases the split has intensified problems and caused an easily discernible rift.

The athletics-physical education split became more pronounced with the advent of Title IX of the Education Amendments of 1972, which forbade sexual discrimination in institutions that accepted federal monies. Because almost all educational institutions are beholden to the federal government for some aspect of their operation, there was hardly an institution that did not have to scrutinize its time-honored, traditionally sex-oriented practices, practices that favored male athletics. Foremost among such practices were perquisites afforded to male athletes but denied to female athletes. Athletic opportunities for females being mandated by the law, the administration of women's athletics could no longer be contained in physical education departments. It was only logical that the women's athletic program come under the aegis of the existing men's athletic program. Consequently the women's athletic program was domiciled in the department of athletics, and in a multitude of instances the final athletics-physical education split was effected.

Just as the physical separation of the two programs had posed problems for the men in an earlier era, so the 1970's saw many problems resulting from the change in administrative operation for women's athletics. The coach-teacher became the primary target for the administrative difficulties promoted by the split. Individuals who had envisioned themselves capable of playing both roles began to realize that the demands placed upon them as recruiter-coaches instead of teacher-coaches were an impossible burden. Many women opted to join their male counterparts as full-time coaches. Still others gave up their coaching responsibilities to devote complete attention to teaching physical education.

The enlarged departments of athletics now have increased their burdens as well as expanded their horizons of opportunity. Because the women's athletic program in the past was not promoted to capture public interest, the financial burden of sponsoring women's athletics has fallen upon the financially vulnerable men's athletic establishment. The burden has not always been accepted with enthusiasm. As a matter of fact, the mandate to give females equal opportunity in athletics often has been ignored. As a result, litigation has followed and in many cases the existing male-dominated department of athletics has been ordered to comply with the law. More optimistically, the 80's suggest that sensitivities to sexual discrimination have been heightened and institutions are mandating change.

Meanwhile many physical education departments are enjoying a new freedom. With the removal of the public performance demands that made it responsible for skill acquisition in sports, dance, aquatics, and gymnastics, the curriculum in physical education can explore dimensions of human vitality neglected in the past. A focus on the art and science of human movement has permitted more diversified approaches to understanding of human activity. Budgets are being used to sponsor a multitude of human movement opportunities that do not culminate in a public performance and that explore intellectual/motoric parameters of human ability.

The public has been slow to adjust to the separation of physical education and athletics and still considers the two so intertwined that one can hardly be distinguished from the other. Thus, as the fortunes of athletics wax, so do the perceived meanings of physical education that are coordinated with the fitness and skill-acquisition emphasis of athletics. As the fortunes of athletics wane, so do the opportunities afforded by physical education classes and the credibility of the practitioners who are physical educators.

What started out as a shared adventure involving the gamut of experience from the novice to the accomplished performer has now separated into two different enterprises with different aims, different participants, different programs, and different practitioners. As the climate of excess comes to bear upon athletics, there are discernible cracks in the structure. Because the system insists that athletics be financially self-sufficient, some desperate coaches and athletic directors are willing to employ practices that are destructive to education. Illegal recruiting, bogus academic credits, slush funds, diminishing academic expectations, and the "washing" of public monies for the athletic program are but a few of the practices that are hurting athletics significantly.

As the athletic establishment reevaluates its program in the 80's, physical education departments will have to be careful that athletics does not become an albatross for the disciplinary integrity of physical education. It need not, if all who are concerned are careful and cooperative rather than careless and combative. Many unexplored schemes await study. As an example there is the possibility of professional sports' investing in sport/aquatic/gymnastic/dance opportunities for the many instead of the few. Such an investment would be undertaken with the expected understanding that the elite would emerge in such a universal program.

Junior high, intermediate, and high schools can stop emulating the college and university pattern of separating athletics and physical education and proceed with carefully identified roles for individuals that suggest cooperative understanding instead of selfish aggrandizement. Some public money needs to be allocated to athletics so that coaches and administrators are not forced to earn the right to explore ability potential. There needs to be a reduction of media involvement in educational athletics so that the temptation of huge monetary gain is removed. In those cases in which media exposure is deemed desirable, the money earned should be used to benefit the entire amateur athletic world instead of lining the coffers of a selected few with media gold. Sharing of the financial gains derived from television contracts could help the entire amateur athletic world.

The unique pattern of amateur athletics in the United States can be used to national advantage if prestigious educators will lend their efforts to sponsoring sanity in sport. Opportunities for those interested in performance need to be expanded instead of restricted. With thoughtful guidance what has been an athletics albatross can take wing and soar to heights. Sound athletic programs for both males and females, in concert with physical education that focuses on the art and science of human movement as the essence of both being and becoming, might truly herald an enriched understanding of the kinesthetic potential of humankind. To such a goal, sanity in sport should subscribe. Sanity in sport must be the watchword of the 80's.

CHAPTER 9

Human Adaptation: Coping Techniques

Linda L. Bain

The individual's ability to adapt to or cope with the environment is a concern in any society. One of the responsibilities of educational institutions is to contribute to the development of adaptation and coping techniques. All areas in the school curriculum share this responsibility, each bringing a unique perspective to it. Physical education's potential contributions are derived from its focus upon movement activities that are expressive and competitive forms of play, and from its commitment to fitness and health.[1] This curriculum area may have particular relevance to certain demands of the environment in the 1980's.

A comprehensive description of contemporary American society cannot be attempted here, but some features are relevant to this discussion. Revolutionized communications technology has altered the political process, the mass culture, and the business world. Technology has not yet produced the predicted increase in leisure time for everyone; instead, it has produced total leisure for a growing population of older adults and unwilling leisure for the unemployed unskilled worker. Racial and ethnic minorities, women, the aging, and the handicapped are struggling to be assimilated into the political and economic mainstream, but also to retain their identity and pride. Political and economic strain and limited natural resources appear to have ended the era of conspicuous consumption. The prevailing mood of the country seems to be pessimism and resignation.

This pessimistic mood is reflected in the ways in which individuals respond to social problems. Responses to one's environment can be described as adaptation or coping. Webster defines adaptation as the adjustment of an organism to its environment, whereas coping is contending with something successfully or being a match for it. Survival requires both behaviors, but amid feelings of resignation and helplessness, coping techniques that emphasize a more active role for the individual in responding to the world may warrant particular attention.

In a physical education program the individual student is an active participant. The observable nature of the tasks makes the learning process more visible and highlights the importance of individual effort and practice in accomplishing a goal. Fitness programs provide students with the opportunity to contribute to their own health and well-being; the popularity of jogging may in part reflect an attempt to regain control over some part of one's life.

Recent research on causal attribution and locus of control has examined the extent to which individuals perceive events to be a consequence of their own actions or due to factors beyond their control.[2] An internal locus of control has been related to a relatively high sense of self-esteem and motivation to learn.[3] People who feel that their actions make a difference are more likely to have high expectations and performance. The conditions under which shifts from external to internal locus of control can be produced are unclear; however, Anshel[4] has suggested that consistent involvement in a personally meaningful task in which feedback is received from an individual whose opinions are respected, could produce such changes. For many children physical education provides such a situation.

What are the implications of this for a physical education program that seeks to encourage children to believe that they can affect events and consequences? Physical education activities should provide success experiences and satisfaction for children with a wide range of abilities. Setting personal goals, discovering individual solutions to problems, adjusting competition to ability level, and participating in group efforts are examples of ways to limit the frustration and embarrassment of individual children. In addition, the feedback provided by the teacher should attribute successes to ability and effort, not to luck or the simplicity of the task ("You did a good job" instead of "Now wasn't that easy?"). Feelings of competence and mastery are the most fundamental of coping techniques.

Another aspect of coping is the ability to maintain appropriate levels of stress in one's life. Stress has been defined as the nonspecific response of the body to demands made upon it.[5] Too much stress can interfere with functioning, but the total lack of stress indicates inadequate stimulation. Human beings attempt to maintain optimal levels of stress, and physical education can contribute to this process.

Exercise appears to decrease one's physiological response to stressors and minimize the occurrence of very high levels of stress, called distress.[6] Involvement in a physical activity also may distract a person from thinking about certain stressors and thereby reduce or delay the onset of a dysfunctional stress response. The teaching of specific relaxation and biofeedback techniques may also enable the person to control stress responses consciously.[7] In situations in which the individual is understimulated, physical activity can be stimulating or stress inducing. This has been particularly useful in the treatment of depression.[8] The fitness component of a physical education program should include a segment on the management of stress.

A third potential contribution of physical education to the development of adaptation and coping techniques is the legitimation of activities that have personal meaning rather than productive worth. In a society in which many individuals spend 10 to 20 years of their adult life retired from work, it is essential that work not be viewed as the only source of personal significance and satisfaction. Physical education, art, and music contribute to leisure education not merely by teaching specific leisure skills, but also by communicating the importance and value of activities that are done for their own sake, for the meaning and enjoyment inherent in the activity rather than for some material gain. Such an affirmation of leisure may become even more critical as leisure time increases and as limits upon materialism are reached.

A physical education program that affirms the validity of leisure emphasizes the importance of activities that students find personally meaningful. Subsequent to a broad and varied elementary school program, the curriculum should consist of a selective program providing in-depth instruction in activities of particular interest to students. The program should provide both instruction and recreation. Instruction without recreation implies that only work-like activities are of sufficient importance to be included in schools. Recreation without instruction implies that physical education activities are not sufficiently serious or important to justify the effort to do them well. Students should have the opportunity to learn specific lifetime activities, but, more important, they should learn to value participation in leisure activities. Administrator and teacher support for athletics but not for physical education communicates that sport is valued as entertainment but that the role of the masses is one of spectator not participant.

Another area that physical education may be able to influence is acceptance of a pluralistic social community. Because of Title IX forbidding sex discrimination in schools and Public Law 94-142 regarding education of the handicapped, the composition of physical education classes now reflects the diversity of the total school population. Erasing the vestiges of discrimination and stereotyping is one of the major challenges facing physical education, particularly because sport is so highly related to sex-role stereotypes.

Several factors affecting social interaction seem specific to physical education. The instructional setting is less formal than most and permits frequent student interaction. Traditionally a high proportion of the activities has involved competition among students. Many of the activities are team efforts involving interdependence of team members. This unique setting requires particular attention to social aspects of the program.

Several approaches are being used to deal with the increasingly heterogeneous physical education classes in ways that emphasize acceptance of all students. Individualized instruction avoids group comparisons and affirms individual worth. Peer teaching establishes supportive relationships among students. Discovery learning communicates acceptance of widely varying solutions to problems. Cooperative "new games" de-emphasize competition between individuals and groups. Designing a physical education program in which all students are included and accepted will not be easy, but if accomplished, it could provide a model of a pluralistic community. The alternative seems to be a reinforcement of present social inequalities.

Several cautions are in order in discussing physical education's contributions to human adaptation and coping techniques. First, these positive outcomes will occur only in certain types of physical education programs. Adaptation and coping techniques tend to be tacit learnings highly dependent upon the manner in which the program is conducted. Although the purpose of the physical education program remains teaching movement activities for the values inherent in those activities, all curriculum areas have an obligation to organize and deliver the instructional program in a manner consistent with the overall purposes of education.

Second, one cannot assume that physical education is the only or the most powerful influence upon any of these adaptation-coping techniques. The family, other curriculum areas, and many other factors will have an influence. Evidence regarding the extent of physical education's impact is not conclusive.

Third, the degree to which learnings in one situation generalize to other situations is unclear. That is, a student may accept minorities in physical education class but not in the neighborhood or on the job. Teachers probably must teach for transfer in order for it to occur.

Despite these cautions physical education seems to have the potential for contributing to the development of human adaptation-coping techniques. The decade of the 1980's will place new demands on all persons, demands that will require individual resilience and strength as well as mutual support and concern. Well-designed physical education programs will contribute to the development of these qualities.

REFERENCES

1. Siedentop, D. *Physical Education: Introductory Analysis.* Dubuque, Iowa: Wm. C. Brown, 1980.

2. de Charms, R. *Personal Causation: The Internal Affective Determinants of Behavior.* New York: Academic Press, 1968.

Phares, E. J. *Locus of Control in Personality.* New York: General Learning Press, 1976.

Weiner, B. *Achievement Motivation and Attribution Theory.* New York: General Learning Press, 1974.

3. Covington, M. V., and Beery, R. G. *Self-Worth and School Learning.* New York: Holt, Rinehart & Winston, 1976.

4. Anshel, M. H. "Effect of Age, Sex and Type of Feedback on Motor Performance and Locus of Control." *Research Quarterly* 50 (1979): 305–317.

5. Selye, H. *Stress Without Distress.* New York: J. B. Lippincott, 1974.

6. deVries, H. A. *Physiology of Exercise.* Dubuque, Iowa: Wm. C. Brown, 1974.

7. Feltz, D. L., and Landers, D. M. "Stress Management Techniques for Sport and Physical Education." *Journal of Physical Education and Recreation* 51, no. 2 (1980): 41–43.

8. Folkins, C. H. "Effects of Physical Training on Mood." *Journal of Clinical Psychology* 32 (1976): 385–388.

Additional Reading

Harris, D. V. *Involvement in Sport: A Somatopsychic Rationale for Physical Activity.* Philadelphia: Lea and Febiger, 1973.

CHAPTER 10

Gym and Gender

March L. Krotee
Nancy L. Struna

[In our seemingly ever-changing world physical educators face a multitude of complex problems. Clearly one significant dilemma to which physical educators, indeed all educators, must attend is the elimination of sexism, the unequal perception of females and males. Social rhetoric and law, especially Title IX of the Education Amendments of 1972 and its implementing regulations of 1975, have mandated that physical educators ensure equality of opportunity, rights, prerogatives, and responsibilities among women and men, girls and boys. Title IX provides that "No person . . . shall, on the basis of sex, be excluded from participation in, be denied the benefits of, or be subjected to discrimination under any education program or activity receiving Federal financial assistance." The regulation implies that the physiological, psychological, and sociological benefits that may be derived from physical education experiences are of equal importance to females and males, and that the experiences necessary to provide these benefits are the same for both males and females. This act seems quite rational, as well as appropriate, given that the varied sex-role assignments distributed to females and males in different cultures suggest that characteristics of femaleness and maleness are not biologically determined; rather, they have been based on cultural definitions of sex-appropriate behavior within the social institution of the epoch.]

Legislative enactment and science are thus squarely on the side of equality of opportunity for both sexes in physical education. Both have provided an answer to the sexism dilemma: eliminate it. Yet as most educators realize, implementing what one knows to be right and justified is not always easy, nor is the way always clear. To be able to write new curriculums and alter facilities and teaching methods, we must understand several factors. We must understand what creates sexual inequality, what social beliefs have fostered it, and why our attitudes have so firmly supported sexual differences that law and science had to be beckoned to reshape them.

Contrary to popular delusions, our contemporary female-male dilemma is not entirely of our own making. We moderns are as much a product of our past as we are of our present, and so too are our habits of and attitudes toward sexual separation. The patterns of primitive societies and the history of Western civilization are replete with examples of sexual differentiations, with ascribed roles and established role models and with individuals and groups who either ignored or defied the lines of gender. If we are to implement equality, as society has mandated, we must understand the roots of inequality as well as the manner in which our predecessors dealt with sexual differences and similarities. In the past of sportsmen and sportswomen, dancers, and other practitioners of physical activity, whether in or outside educational institutions, lie not only some causes and rationales for our current dilemma, but also some concepts and processes that we need to consider in proposing change.

Gender distinctions are rooted in the needs and beliefs of ancient, medieval, and early modern Western cultures. In retrospect we can believe that the causes were legion and that most, if not all, arose from need. Whether because of human nature or the nature of society, humans needed to distinguish themselves from others, to order society, to establish a division of labor, to honor the gods, and to survive and establish subsequent generations. These needs led to beliefs: that some men were different from other men and, of course, from women; that society was organized hierarchically on the basis of these differences; and that certain individuals or groups could most adequately perform certain specialized functions. In a sense, then, the development of a "second sex" or the development of differences between men and women, as well as the development of differences among men, arose from and nurtured the nature of ordered societies whose members assumed or achieved specialized roles largely dependent upon both need and belief.

Throughout the ancient, medieval, and early modern Western cultures, these needs for and beliefs in individuals' distinctiveness, and consequently gender distinctiveness, affected sport and physical training. The Spartans, military conquerors of the Grecian peninsula, separated their children by sex after the age of seven, for military training and for physical and psychosocial training associated with bearing children for service to the state. Spartan women were expected to engage in physical activity, including gymnastics and dance, to ensure the production of healthy, preferably male offspring. Male officials of Panhellenic games and the ancient Olympic Games, sacred religious festivals conducted in honor of the reigning deities Apollo, Poseidon, and Zeus, refused to allow women either to participate actively or to view the naked male athlete. However, Tryphosa, a female, broke the Greek feminite arete while capturing the one-stade footrace at the Pythian and Isthmian Games.

Later societies also established role models based on sex, which were reflected in sport. Medieval knights performed in tilts and melees while female admirers observed. Perhaps only Joan of Arc ever crossed the bounds of the male militarism and knightly endeavor that these activities fostered. Even in Tudor and Stuart England, scholars scribed civility manuals for young noblemen, and young men and boys learned horsemanship and were trained with sword and bow, while women remained in the background. Only when a woman assumed the mantle of national leadership and exercised her prerogatives as head of state did sexual lines in sport temporarily blur. Such a woman was Elizabeth I, Queen of England, who participated in festivals and sport with her courtiers.

Although the eras mentioned above show some exceptions, the belief was generally held by the religious, political, and intellectual elite that certain social tasks required special talents and skills that were defined by gender. However, the evidence suggests that when a woman was born into, bred for, or happened upon traditionally male responsibilities, she could carry them out. Still, as time passed, needs and beliefs became traditions, and these operated against any regular crossing of gender lines among the social elite.

On the other hand, outside institutionalized history, people who generally did not make decisions affecting society's organization, political orientation, or religious doctrine found ways to overcome or ignore some sexual differences. Whether in work or in day-to-day training, peasants, yeomen, taverners, and others in a variety of occupations attended less to sexual distinctions than to completing a task, surviving, rearing a family, and sporting. In ancient as well as in early modern societies, women and men worked side by side in the fields, and boys and girls played games, ran races, and danced. In ceremonial and initiation rites, of course, lines between the sexes remained, but on a daily basis the same lines blurred. In contrast to the elites, commoners generally needed to strike a natural balance between traditional dichotomies—master and servant, father and son or mother and daughter, and male and female.

Perhaps as late as the nineteenth century, the bulk of Western civilization's members maintained this natural balance in their daily lives. In America through the colonial period, the mass of settlers lived and learned, as had their ancestors, with some duties for men, some for women, and some for both. As children, girls and boys learned to ride horses by imitating their parents. New England adults joined work and sport in husking bees, while Southerners learned to shoot, paddle canoes, and gamble with little apparent effort to rationalize and to justify what men could do and women could not, or vice versa. Common colonial Americans accomplished their tasks, acquired and transmitted knowledge and attitudes, and sported, both on the basis of sex and regardless of sex.

This natural balance between sex-dependent and sex-independent activities had developed among people who were relatively isolated and whose livelihoods were relatively simple and mundane, at least by today's standards. Cultural change had occurred, of course, and society had become more sophisticated and complex as one age had been molded into the next. Still, on the surface, the basic needs and beliefs of common people remained fairly stable and tradition bound. For several centuries before 1800, however, the roots of radical and eventually rapid change had been sown and nurtured. These blossomed in the nineteenth century, and their effects changed not only the face of American culture but also the natural balance between sex-dependent and sex-independent attitudes and actions so long maintained by society.

In the nineteenth century, the influence of intellectuals, specialized industrial labor, Victorian moral notions, and the institutionalization of education combined to thwart the natural balance between men's and women's spheres and human responsibility. Both needs and beliefs altered, and these four elements were at once causes of change and sources of alternative attitudes and actions. To be sure, all four had existed in one form or another in preceding societies, but not until the nineteenth century, especially by the middle of the century, did they mature and mesh, foster one another, and affect the nature of society so significantly.

Intellectual elites, industrialization, and Victorian morality joined to instigate, rationalize, and ascribe meaning to the magnificent changes that catapulted the United States into the forefront of the world's prosperous, forward-looking, and single-minded nations. Intellectuals and businessmen alike emphasized two older concepts, social hierarchy (the "great chain of being") and maleness, and combined them in an explanation for and a moral resulting from the nation's successful industrial expansion and raised standard of living. Free, white males thus not only inherited the earth but also emerged as the Darwinian favorite upon whom survival of the nation depended. At the same time the conception of women as preservers of the "flower" of humanity solidified. In imitation of England's nearly ageless sovereign, Queen Victoria, women propelled themselves or were propelled by others into this progressive society as individuals with distinguishable roles, both symbolic and real—emblems of fragility, matrons of man's sacred honor, marble busts on the pedestal of human achievement, and, of course, wives and mothers perpetuating the family institution, seamstresses, and teachers of future leaders.

For these attitudes to spread among the democracy, they had to be codified and transmitted to those who aspired to share in the wealth, knowledge, and morality of America. The key to ensuring a liberal, progressive, enterprising citizenry lay in the eradication of unenlightened, unhealthy, unscientific, and immoral beliefs and actions through formal education in the schools. By the middle of the nineteenth century, then, the school, though obviously not new, did complete its assumption of educational responsibilities from more traditional agencies such as the family, the church, the taverns, and the community. In the school, whether at first the common school or eventually public and private colleges and high schools, children and adolescents learned to read, cipher, prepare for an occupation, and become healthy, upstanding, competitive Americans. Enter the physical educator.

The evolution of the specialized, formally trained physical educator was long and arduous. Training in and through the physical had always existed; thus acceptance of the idea and the need was less problematic than were the development and systematizing of how and when. Formal school experiences directed first by advocates and eventually by professionals evolved through a series of exercises in manual labor practices, in gymnastics, and eventually in sport and dance. Those who perceived themselves as intellectual leaders, especially New England Brahmins and preservers of the plantation mystique, initially provided physical training for their own kind. Men taught boys, and women taught girls, for this was in keeping with their enlightened, specialized notions of themselves and their designs for posterity. Viewed as both successful and necessary for all Americans, especially for the maintenance of health and "Americanization," schools expanded and provided for physical culture either in recess periods or free time and gradually in gymnasium coursework.

Throughout the latter half of the nineteenth century, the development of the school concurrent with the broadening influence of intellectuals, the specialization of industrial labor, and the acceptance of Victorian morality, helps to explain the initial distinctiveness of genders in gymnasiums. Schools oriented to intellectual and occupational training of either men or women for their specialized roles in a progressive and enlightened industrial society provided physical training, eventually physical education, on the same model—separation by sex. Through the late nineteenth and early twentieth centuries, male and female educators, especially in colleges and universities, enforced what had become traditional in education: men and women learned about and participated in sport and dance in separate classes and on separate teams. Educational leaders such as Amy Morris Homans, Dudley Sargeant, and their disciples spread this doctrine throughout the land with the help of other anthropometrists, physicians, gymnastics "systems" advocates, and students themselves. A plethora of socioscientific educational rationales for the continuation of these sex distinctions emerged. As it had in the past, need had led to belief, and the educational system, the great American equalizer, had conserved both.

At this juncture, the late nineteenth and early twentieth centuries, the current of cultural change moved society away from its propensity to separate the sexes, toward integration. As a reaction to their own industrial achievement and to Victorian constraints, as well as to other cultural phenomena such as wars, some men and women realized that separation had benefited neither; in fact, one may argue, total sexual separation had never existed. Regardless of the precise cause, the fact remains that the propensity toward gender separation was beginning, ever so slightly, to fade, and opportunities appeared for women to engage in sport and physical activity either primarily or secondarily. The late nineteenth century development of the sporting and country club and the development of horse racing, boxing, and baseball into full-blown spectator events vied for the attention of the modern woman. Women found opportunity for participation in amateur, professional, and recreational pursuits, and by 1910 industry began to provide time and physical activities for the female employee. Even the all-male Olympic Games fell prey to the swift current, much to the dismay of Baron Pierre de Coubertin. In Stockholm in 1908 Gwendolyn Eastlake-Smith from Great Britain captured the first gold medal for women and legitimately launched women into the Games. By World War I female athletes and teams were being vigorously sought to travel and compete internationally.

In effect, from just before the turn of the century society provided opportunities for interaction, though clearly not immediately for equal participation, between men and women. Barriers and stereotypes remained, but they were attacked and weakened by wars, a human response to genuine ability, and eventually a sense of sharing among minorities, especially women, Blacks, and special populations. One cannot ignore a Babe Didrikson, Philip Wrigley's All-American Girls' Baseball League, an Althea Gibson, or a Billie Jean King, all of whom found support from society in general, although their support was qualitatively less than for a Babe Ruth, the Yankees, an Arnold Palmer, or a Jimmy Connors.

Compared to the attitudes and actions of physical educators who continued to support sex-segregated programs, the progressive reintegration of men and women in society represented a successful attempt to reestablish a natural balance between sex-dependent and sex-independent rights and responsibilities once visible among Americans' agrarian-based ancestors. The process has been difficult, bitter, and rife with discrepancies, and it apparently is not complete. Yet, again compared to what has been and in some cases what remains current in educational circles, society as a whole has been infinitely more encouraging about eventual elimination of sexism.

In keeping with the traditional relationship between society and education, then, educators must at least follow society's lead. Society, via its climate of opinion, its value structure, and its legal system, has mandated that the profession of education respond to the most current needs and beliefs, which are dependent upon sexual equality. It would be more than appropriate if educators in general and physical educators in particular would shed their traditional role as conservators of society's mores and values and take the vanguard in achieving balance between the sexes in our present physical activity and sport models. Let us lead through example in the gymnasiums and on the playing fields and thrust our profession into a position of leadership in what some have characterized as the emancipation of the female.

This position is not radical or revolutionary in nature. "Revolution" connotes substantial alteration in the institutional structure, authority relationships, and ideological definitions of society, often accomplished through conflict and violence. Examples of revolution include the Russian Revolution of 1917 and those in Cuba and China. Instead of revolution, in which massive and most often radical changes are initiated, we are referring to the rights, privileges, and openness of sharing and participating in the experiences and potential benefits of human movement. We are also referring to the removal of the physiological and psychosocial chains and barriers that now exist in our classrooms, in our gymnasiums, and on our playing fields. These barriers may be thought of as impediments to the educational socialization process, educational equality, and attainment of status. Certainly more than modest strides have been taken in these directions through the enactment of Title IX of the Education Amendments of 1972; however, there is much work to do in exploring alternatives to separate classes and departments and dissimilar curriculums, teaching methods, and teaching styles.

Perhaps the greatest challenge for physical educators of the 80's is to dispel many of the taboos, myths, and prejudices concerning the sexes that

90

have long served to limit women's realization of their full potential for wholesome participation in physical activity and sport. Social myths and practices such as the identification of the female with nature and a lower order of existence; the perception of the woman as passive, submissive, private, and subordinate; and giving to the female less choice or opportunity in regard to physical activity must be discarded. These myths and practices must be replaced by systematic scientific inquiry into the physiological and psychosocial ramifications of individuals as they interact with their environment in pursuit of wholesome physical activity. The research must focus not only on the systematic gathering of data, but also on delivery mechanisms so that the practitioner may be sensitized to the accurate issues and concerns of gender integration in physical activity and sport. The practitioner needs and deserves much more than confrontation with events. He or she needs to include research perceptions and be assured of their availability on later occasions. This availability is dependent on at least two factors: first, the individual's discovery of personal meaning, and second, the satisfaction of need.

The research and its corresponding integration into curriculum, teaching methods, and teaching styles should focus on building a positive view of the self, opening the mind and body to new experiences regarding movement, and sharing these experiences with others in a manner that develops the total individual, physically and psychosocially, to his or her fullest potential. This potential includes the formation of skills, habits, beliefs, and values for effective and wholesome participation in physical activity that ultimately rearms and reforms the socialization process.

Research should also be conducted on girls' and women's participation in physical activity and sport. This research might include data on the biophysical limitations of the female participant and the effects of chronic physical activity on early childhood menstruation and pregnancy, as well as updated and accurate information concerning body composition, strength, and endurance. The myriad of psychosocial ramifications must also be delved into to reflect the totality of our integrative society, including both sexes, the aged, and special populations. This research base will dispel the inaccuracies, prejudices, and myths of the past and serve to guide physical educators of the 80's in building sound curriculum and instructional approaches to the physical and psychosocial integration of the sexes in the classroom, in the gymnasium, and on the playing field.

There is no longer any reason or excuse for society's failing to provide equal resources for physical activity, including curriculum, budgets, facilities, and leadership to ensure equal opportunity for all. As physical educators we endorse the right of equal opportunity and hope that sound experiences in human movement will help shape the future of society and lead to a more healthy and wholesome quality of life.

REFERENCES

Association for Supervision and Curriculum Development. *Perceiving, Behaving, Becoming. The 1962 Yearbook of the Association for Supervision and Curriculum Development.* Washington, D.C.: Author, 1962.

Beecher, C. *Letters to the People on Health and Happiness.* New York: Harper, 1855.

Blaufarb, M. *Title IX of the Education Amendments of 1972: A Manual on Physical Education and Sports Programs for Administrators, Athletic Directors, Coaches, and Teachers in Local Education Agencies and for Personnel in General Physical Education Programs in Colleges and Universities.* Washington, D.C.: United States Department of Health, Education and Welfare, Office of Education, 1976.

Cogswell, J. C., and Bancroft, G. *Prospectus of a School to Be Established at Round Hill, Northampton, Massachusetts.* Cambridge, Mass.: 1823.

de Beauvoir, S. *The Second Sex.* New York: Alfred A. Knopf, 1953.

Dewey, J. *Experience and Education.* New York: MacMillan, 1938.

Freeman, J. *Women: A Feminist Perspective.* Palo Alto, Calif.: Mayfield Publishing Co., 1975.

Gerber, E. "The Controlled Development of Collegiate Sport for Women, 1923–1936." *Journal of Sport History* 2 (1975): 1–28.

Gerber, E. W.; Felshin, J.; Berlin, P.; and Wyrick, W. *The American Woman in Sport.* Reading, Mass.: Addison-Wesley, 1974.

Gulick, L. *Physical Education by Muscular Exercise.* Philadelphia: P. Blakiston's Son and Co., 1904.

Harris, D. V. *Involvement in Sport: A Somatopsychic Rationale for Physical Activity.* Philadelphia: Lea and Febiger, 1973.

Harris, H. A. *Greek Athletes and Athletics.* Bloomington, Ind.: Indiana University Press, 1966.

Hill, L. *Athletic and Out-Door Sports for Women.* New York: MacMillan, 1903.

Holliman, J. *American Sports (1785–1835).* Durham, N.C.: The Seeman Press, 1931.

Kahlick, E.; Papp, L. G.; and Subert, Z. *Olympic Games 1896–1972.* Budapest, Hungary: Zrinyi Printing House, 1972.

Katz, M., ed. *Education in American History.* New York: Praeger Publishers, 1973.

Krotee, M. L. *The Dimensions of Sport Sociology.* West Point, N.Y.: Leisure Press, 1979.

_____. "Issues and Problems of the Olympic Games." Paper presented to the Sport Philosophy and Sport Sociology Academies of the National Association of Sport and Physical Education, Detroit, Michigan, April 1980.

_____. "The Psychological Effects of Training and Conditioning." In *Sport Psychology,* edited by R. Mechikoff. Duluth, Minn.: University of Minnesota, Duluth Press, 1979.

_____. "The Rise and Demise of Sport: A Reflection of Uruguayan Society." *The Annals of the American Academy of Political and Social Science* 445 (1979): 141–154.

_____. "Sociological Perspectives of the Olympic Movement." In *Toward a Social Philosophy of the Olympics,* edited by J. Seagrave and D. Chu. Champaign, Ill.: Human Kinetics Press, in press.

_____, and West, P. "The Psychosocial Dimensions of Women in Sport." In *Sport Psychology,* edited by R. Mechikoff. Duluth, Minn.: University of Minnesota, Duluth Press, 1979.

Lee, M. "The Case For and Against Intercollegiate Athletics for Women and the Situation Since 1923." *Research Quarterly* 2 (1931): 93–127.

Lewis, G. "Sport and the Making of American Higher Education: The Early Years, 1783–1875." In *73rd Proceedings,* National College Physical Education Association for Men, December 1970, pp. 208–213.

Lucas, J., and Smith, R. *Saga of American Sport.* Philadelphia: Lea and Febiger, 1978.

Oglesby, C. *Women and Sport: From Myth to Reality.* Philadelphia: Lea and Febiger, 1978.

Ortner, S. "Is Female to Male As Nature Is to Culture?" In *Women, Culture and Society,* edited by M. Rosaldo and L. Lamphere. Palo Alto, Calif.: Stanford University Press, 1973.

Spears, B., and Swanson, R. *History of Sport and Physical Activity in the United States.* Dubuque, Iowa: Wm. C. Brown, 1978.

Struna, N. *The Cultural Significance of Sport in the Colonial Chesapeake and Massachusetts.* Unpublished doctoral dissertation, University of Maryland, 1979.

_____. "Sport and Colonial Education." Paper presented to the History Academy of the National Association of Sport and Physical Education, Kansas City, Missouri, April 1978.

Woody, T. *Life and Education in Early Societies.* New York: MacMillan, 1949.

CHAPTER 11

Human Development: Articulations with Health, Recreation, Dance, Safety, and Gerontology

Celeste Ulrich

Most areas of knowledge are derived from already existing disciplines. As a discipline is studied and analyzed, it usually becomes apparent that more needs to be known about a particular subdivision under study. As knowledge in that subdivision proliferates and suggests new ideas, a new area of knowledge develops that has the potential for discrete disciplinary integrity. With physical education this process was not enacted.

Instead, physical education was generated because of evidence that the physical aspects of human behavior needed attention. Medicine was already attentive to the unwell, the disabled, the infirm. It became physical education's concern to suggest techniques that would not only prevent malfunction and ineffectuality but also assist the individual in becoming all that he or she could become. Thus physical education became a pattern of education that explored and promoted physical activity and used gymnastics and games for a variety of reasons, the maintenance of good health being among the most important.

As a result of physical education's health motif, an interest grew in the understanding of health practices that would alleviate sickness. Originally these practices dealt with the hygiene of the individual. Nutrition, rest, relaxation, accident prevention, exercise, cleanliness, were some of the facets of hygiene that were emphasized. It was natural that such programs should be allied with programs in physical education because most of the concepts that were explored reflected motoric and affective behaviors rather than cognitive insights. For many years physical education and hygiene were intertwined both in the school curriculum and in public consciousness. Activity forms were strongly hygiene oriented to produce strength and endurance. Hygiene understandings were embedded in education about bodily function, function that had greater integrity when overt activity was employed.

As hygiene slowly evolved into the larger concept of health, material was amassed that extended understandings beyond the individual's adjustment to environment and looked at community efforts to sponsor what was known as "good health." Soon "individual and community health" courses took the place of the old hygiene courses and began to manifest themselves as entities separate from physical education.

Physical education was also beginning to lean away from a single focus on the maintenance of individual hygiene and using activity for behavioral change and social interaction. The gradual drift intensified as physical educators began to study movement on its own merits instead of for its end results. Physical educators interested in health began to subdivide their concerns about human well-being into specialized courses on reproduction, nutrition, drug usage, and other specific aspects of the human's interface with the environment. During this time, as a result of the concern, a number of physical educators began to focus their interest on the meaning of health to the individual and the community, and began to build constructs to distinguish health education as a field of inquiry in its own right. They began to identify themselves as health/physical educators.

In addition to the natural split between health and physical education that emerged as a result of different focuses, a deepening of the abyss between the two areas was brought about by practitioners in health who no longer felt comfortable as physical educators and began to identify themselves exclusively as health educators. They believed they were divorced from the medical professions by virtue of their interest in wellness rather than sickness. Thus health and physical education began to travel different paths, with different advocates, along the route to human well-being.

Not too long after the difference between health and physical education became manifest, yet another group emerged within physical education that was increasingly disenchanted with physical education's attention to the school-age individual. The people in this group suggested that not only were many individuals desirous of activity patterns built on a play motif, but also some significant times were being ignored. They contended that physical educators had concentrated all of their interest on the time span of the school's responsibilities. Thus the school day (from 9:00 a.m. to 3:00 p.m.), the school week (from Monday through Friday), and the school year (from September until June) were commanding the attention of physical educators. But what was being done for people at other times, in what this group was beginning to identify as leisure time? Individuals needed guided activity plans for after school, for the weekend, for summer vacation. Thus a sizable group of physical educators began to study the feasibility of activity during leisure, in places other than the school, by people of all ages—a plan of recreation. This primary group was joined by others outside physical education who saw physical activity patterns as being the core of recreation's concern but not the *only* focus. To the traditional recreation program of sports and games were added programs in nature, crafts, outdoor living, camping, and many other activities that could be performed during leisure time. Then, just as the health educators had done before them, the recreationalists began to push a unique concept of recreation. Such a concept, they contended, necessitated knowledge regarding how recreation could and should be organized within the community, and the interweaving of all of the community's resources to improve recreation.

Recreationalists began to feel that their focus was sufficiently different from physical education's to warrant a unique curriculum and to start to bring together all of those people who had expressed an interest in "the worthy use of leisure time." National organizations were formed to assist the recreation experts and to help influence the government to conserve resources (both human and environmental) to encourage popular support of national commitments to social goals.

Thus did physical education spawn health and recreation. In addition, a unique movement form in physical education had a long and distinguished history as an entity and felt its horizons to be limited as a part of the physical education program. That movement form was dance. The dancers (many of whom were public performers) were not sure that dance should be contained in the vacuum of formal education. They insisted that theirs was a long history of public performance for all ages at all times. In addition, dance was a form of self-expression and was only minimally interested in the healthful outcomes of performance. The dancers resisted being relegated to physical education, whose primary focus was fitness rather than expression. However, the dancers conceded that the placement of dance in departments of physical education was a more natural alliance than with any other conceptual chunk of knowledge because dance was based upon human movement patterns.

But if the subject matter of physical education was proliferating, so too was the new health concept. A group of people began to spin off from what was just beginning to be acknowledged as the health area. These individuals saw concern with stress prevention as the major obligation of health for human well-being. Stress prevention, they argued, could be in terms of individual adaptive techniques or in mastering the technicalities of the environment, an environment that was changing very rapidly. The advent of the automobile had brought about revolutionary change, and it was apparent that education had to be directed at drivers in the form of driver education. Accident prevention was another pattern of stress prevention that these individuals identified, and they contended there was also a need to learn how to handle individuals who had been victimized by accidents. Thus there was the need to understand first-aid techniques. The area of stress prevention soon began to be identified as safety. The safety educators, like the health educators before them, became increasingly uneasy about being subsumed under a parent concern that would not allow them to explore fully their specialized interests, and they started to look for ways to move out of health's center of concern.

Today another group of people is allying itself with physical education, health, recreation, dance, and safety. These people have an interest in the age group designated as "elders," and they are attempting to locate a home where they feel that their multidisciplinary interests will best be served. The gerontologists have had difficulty in standing alone in the midst of academic organization; at the same time they have not felt comfortable in schools of education or social services. They believe that their concern about the aging process transcends a single arena of action. There is some indication that gerontology feels comfortable as a part of the multifaceted endeavor of physical education, health, recreation, dance, and safety. This comfort is not so much in identification with human movement potential or in identification with physical well-being or in identification with self-actualization during leisure time (which may be the majority of time for the elderly). Instead, gerontologists express satisfaction in being a part of a group of people who have multidisciplinary concerns and who have had various degrees of difficulty in being totally acceptable in the academic world. Gerontologists, like physical educators, health educators, recreationalists, dancers, and safety educators, are concerned with a holistic understanding of human behavior instead of concentration on cognitive patterns.

Numerous other groups are standing on the periphery ready to emerge as full-blown interests. Individuals in the aquatic faction of human performance are poised to proclaim their specialty as distinct, much as the dancers have. Those interested in sport have already suggested that their specialized interest is so demanding that it can no longer be accommodated within the larger whole of physical education. Soon the gymnasts will proclaim their need for more specialized attention. Individuals interested solely in drugs are already moving away from the health specialists, and the area encompassing birth control, reproduction, and infant and child care is suggesting that it has more to teach than is allowed in traditional patterns of health education. As the production of knowledge is intensified and as individuals become intrigued with unique aspects of knowledge, undoubtedly parent conceptual groups will spawn additional groups ready to declare their independence from their conceptual family unit.

As a matter of fact, the old family model is now proving to be anathema to some of the groups identified. Each wishes to be visible and to seek autonomy and a degree of independence in specific organizational structures. The family model that suggests physical education as parent also suggests that growing children need to free themselves from parental control and direct parental influence.

Of late, there is ample evidence of discomfort on the part of health, recreation, and dance that too close an association with the parent physical education can both inhibit and smother. Safety has evidenced the same attitude toward health education, and gerontology is wary lest it become enmeshed in a web that will trap its unique multidisciplinary perspective and snare its energy in a good-health matrix.

At present the family model that many envision as encompassing the six areas of physical education, health, recreation, dance, safety, and gerontology, might look like Figure 1.

FIGURE 1.

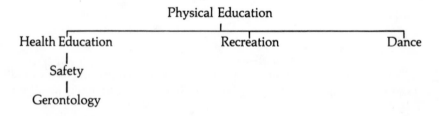

Although such a model might explain how the various areas of concern were conceived and may even suggest the relative size of each component, it need no longer be accepted as a viable operational model. Instead, it might be wise to mutate the family model from that of parent and children to that of sibling interaction. Such a family paradigm tacitly assumes that each component is unique and discrete but a common link holds the components together.

Literally hundreds of people have attempted to find the word that will best identify what is common to the enterprise, but no one has yet been successful. It seems glaringly apparent that *the* word will emerge, a word

FIGURE 2.

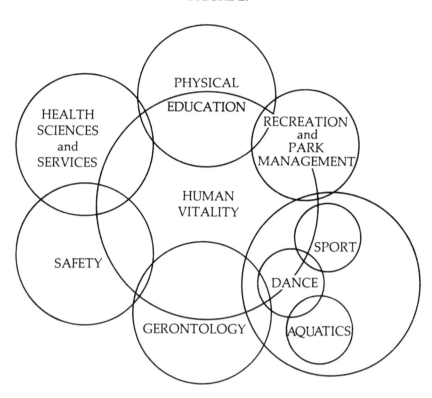

that will allow us to name departments/schools/colleges and make us all feel akin to one another in an alliance with a meaningful family identification.

Some of the words identified have been newly coined such as "soc-psychkinetic"; other tags have used concepts that tend to be universal such as human performance, kinetic arts and sciences, kinesiology, human and community development, wellness. Clearly the final word has not yet been identified, but it might be possible to assume that the word will convey movement, elan, well-being, self-actualization, and physiological integrity, a vitality of human function and purpose. Using the word "vitality" as the beginning of an idea, I propose that the current family paradigm might be depicted as in Figure 2.

In the above model it is possible to change the position of the interacting components of vitality as well as to change the size of the circles.

Recreation and health are clearly growing at a very rapid rate. Physical education, on the other hand, seems to be holding firm and enriching what exists rather than adding to its holdings. The above model allows and even generates mutation that will accommodate variability and differing social/political emphases.

Clearly all of the components of vitality interact on the themes of total fitness, play behavior, human performance, and adaptation. Those four themes can permit formulation of the human development design to focus more attention on the whole person and the development of the whole person to his or her fullest potential.

There may be some feeling that physical education has lost its power position as it has moved into a relationship in which power is, more realistically, shared rather than delegated. Such a feeling does not recognize the true strength that can be engendered by numerous components subscribing to four significant themes as they contribute to a kinship in human vitality.

The historical development of physical education left physical educators in a quandary. It was difficult to know exactly who we were, what we were doing, and with what we were working. The subsequent analysis of physical education with sensitivity to the changes that have occurred, is bringing into lucid focus the real subject matter of physical education and the place that physical education has in the confounding puzzle of human understanding. The current design establishes with greater clarity the supporting roles of all of human vitality's related areas. Such a pattern has the potential to foster a richer design than any that has been known in the past and a stronger and more flexible conceptual fabric that will not ravel, shred, or shrink. To be alert to human existence is no longer enough. It is our obligation to be truly sensitive to the elan of that existence, the vitality of human life. It is a charge that has the warp and woof of meaning for physical education in the 80's.

The physical education pattern of the 80's promises to be different from anything we have known in the past. There will be stress on the integrated individual and that person's responsibility for self-movement-management. There will be emphasis upon total fitness to accommodate well-being. There will be a process- and product-designed curriculum that is attentive to motor skill acquisition, the social aspects of human development, and individual adaptation. There will be an effort to resolve the differences dividing athletics and physical education and to bring sanity to sport even as physical education is enriched.

The 80's usher in exciting opportunities for the "now" physical education. The theory has been expounded. Physical educators need only put that theory into practice.

The Contributors

Linda L. Bain is Associate Professor of Physical Education at the University of Houston, Texas. Dr. Bain achieved instant attention when she published "The Hidden Curriculum," which studied the covert patterns of curriculum as contrasted with the overt claims espoused. She is a nationwide speaker on curriculum ideas and humanistic educational practices.

Lynn A. Barnett is Assistant Professor at the University of Illinois, working in the Leisure Behavior Research Laboratory. Professor Barnett's keen interest in play theory has been highlighted by research in cognitive development through play and arousal seeking and information processing in play. She is currently associate editor of *Leisure Sciences*.

Elizabeth S. Bressan is Assistant Professor of Physical Education at the University of Oregon. She has taught at the University of Kentucky and the University of Wisconsin-LaCrosse. Besides curriculum and elementary physical education, her interests extend to the philosophical constructs of physical education.

Ann E. Jewett is head of the Division of Health, Physical Education and Recreation at the University of Georgia, Athens. She is widely recognized as a curriculum theorist in physical education and is a well-known lecturer. She and her students have developed a taxonomy for the motor domain of human behavior that is used widely. Dr. Jewett's concern with futurism has been encapsulated in the 14th Amy Morris Homans Lecture, sponsored by the National Association for Physical Education in Higher Education.

March L. Krotee is a member of the faculty of the Division of Physical Education and Coordinator of the Physical Activity Program at the University of Minnesota. Dr. Krotee is Past Chairperson of the Sport Sociology Academy of the National Association of Sport and Physical Education, serves as Regional Coordinator for the North American Society for the Sociology of Sport, and is a Fellow in the Research Consortium of the American Alliance for Health, Physical Education, Recreation and Dance. He has published several texts, including *The Dimensions of Sport*

Sociology, has lectured and presented numerous papers concerning the psychosocial and psychophysiological parameters of sport and physical activity, and has been awarded honors by the governments of Brazil, Mexico, and Uruguay for his contributions to sport service and physical education.

Alexander W. McNeill is Associate Professor of Physical Education at the University of Idaho, Moscow. Dr. McNeill is known for his innovative thinking in the area of applied physiology and biomechanics. He has published research on behavioral and biological factors involved in exercise and strenuous activity.

Virginia Martens Hayes operates her own business, Peak Health Products, in Houston, Texas. Her interest has sponsored her investigation of the transcendental theme of human endeavor, and she has paid special attention to what is called "the peak-experience in sport." She is interested in further exploration of the physiological and psychological correlates of human behavior in connection with human movement patterns.

Anne L. Rothstein is Associate Professor of Physical Education at Herbert H. Lehman College of the City University of New York, Bronx. Her editorship of the publication *Theory into Practice* has provided a scholarly dimension to the area of motor behavior, and she is highly regarded for the translation of motoric paradigms into meaning for practitioners. Rothstein is a frequent lecturer in the area of motor learning and control.

Nancy L. Struna is a member of the faculty of the Division of Physical Education at the University of Minnesota. Dr. Struna is a member of the North American Society of Sport History, the American Historical Association, the Organization of American Historians, and the History of Sport Academy of the National Association of Sport and Physical Education. She has presented papers concerning the historical development of sport and physical activity at international and national levels and is a recipient of the Most Outstanding Women in America award.

Celeste Ulrich is Dean of the College of Health, Physical Education, Recreation, Dance and Gerontology at the University of Oregon, Eugene. Dr. Ulrich's areas of expertise include stress physiology, behavioral bases of human movement, and the significance and meaning of physical education. She has published numerous books and articles in all of these areas. She is a former president of both the National Association of Physical Education for College Women and the American Alliance for Health, Physical Education, Recreation and Dance, and is a well-known speaker and consultant.

LeRoy T. Walker is currently Professor of Physical Education at North Carolina Central University in Durham. He served as national coach of the United States Track and Field Team during the 1976 Olympiad and is internationally accepted as one of the foremost track and field consultants in the world. Dr. Walker's teaching interests have included human movement potential and physical education for the atypical, as well as the specific, movement forms of sport. He is a former president of the American Alliance for Health, Physical Education, Recreation and Dance and has been cited by numerous organizations for exemplary service to humankind and for disciplinary excellence in education.